HARDY
BORDER

Edited

H. H. THOMAS

First published in 1921

This edition published by Read Books Ltd.
Copyright © 2019 Read Books Ltd.
This book is copyright and may not be
reproduced or copied in any way without
the express permission of the publisher in writing

British Library Cataloguing-in-Publication Data
A catalogue record for this book is available
from the British Library

A Short History of Gardening

Gardening is the practice of growing and cultivating plants as part of horticulture more broadly. In most domestic gardens, there are two main sets of plants; 'ornamental plants', grown for their flowers, foliage or overall appearance – and 'useful plants' such as root vegetables, leaf vegetables, fruits and herbs, grown for consumption or other uses. For many people, gardening is an incredibly relaxing and rewarding pastime, ranging from caring for large fruit orchards to residential yards including lawns, foundation plantings or flora in simple containers. Gardening is separated from farming or forestry more broadly in that it tends to be much more labour-intensive; involving active participation in the growing of plants.

Home-gardening has an incredibly long history, rooted in the 'forest gardening' practices of prehistoric times. In the gradual process of families improving their immediate environment, useful tree and vine species were identified, protected and improved whilst undesirable species were eliminated. Eventually foreign species were also selected and incorporated into the 'gardens.' It was only after the emergence of the first civilisations that wealthy individuals began to create gardens for aesthetic purposes. Egyptian tomb paintings from around 1500 BC provide some of the earliest physical evidence of ornamental horticulture and landscape design; depicting lotus ponds surrounded by symmetrical rows of acacias and palms. A notable example of an ancient ornamental garden was the 'Hanging Gardens of Babylon' – one of the Seven Wonders of the Ancient World.

Ancient Rome had dozens of great gardens, and Roman estates tended to be laid out with hedges and vines and contained a wide variety of flowers – acanthus, cornflowers, crocus, cyclamen, hyacinth, iris, ivy, lavender, lilies, myrtle, narcissus, poppy, rosemary and violets as well as statues and sculptures. Flower beds were also popular in the courtyards of rich Romans. The Middle Ages represented a period of decline for gardens with aesthetic purposes however. After the fall of Rome gardening was done with the purpose of growing medicinal herbs and/or decorating church altars. It was mostly monasteries that carried on the tradition of garden design and horticultural techniques during the medieval period in Europe. By the late thirteenth century, rich Europeans began to grow gardens for leisure as well as for medicinal herbs and vegetables. They generally surrounded them with walls – hence, the 'walled garden.'

These gardens advanced by the sixteenth and seventeenth centuries into symmetrical, proportioned and balanced designs with a more classical appearance. Gardens in the renaissance were adorned with sculptures (in a nod to Roman heritage), topiary and fountains. These fountains often contained 'water jokes' – hidden cascades which suddenly soaked visitors. The most famous fountains of this kind were found in the Villa d'Este (1550-1572) at Tivoli near Rome. By the late seventeenth century, European gardeners had started planting new flowers such as tulips, marigolds and sunflowers.

These highly complex designs, largely created by the aristocracy slowly gave way to the individual gardener however – and this is where this book comes in! Cottage Gardens first emerged during the Elizabethan times, originally created by poorer workers to provide themselves with food and herbs, with flowers planted amongst them for decoration. Farm workers were generally provided with cottages set in a small garden—about an acre—where they could grow food, keep pigs, chickens and often bees; the latter necessitating the planting of decorative pollen flora. By Elizabethan times there was more prosperity, and thus more room to grow flowers. Most of the early cottage garden flowers would have had practical uses though —violets were spread on the floor (for their pleasant scent and keeping out vermin); calendulas and primroses were both attractive and used in cooking. Others, such as sweet william and hollyhocks were grown entirely for their beauty.

Here lies the roots of today's home-gardener; further influenced by the 'new style' in eighteenth century England which replaced the more formal, symmetrical 'Garden à la française'. Such gardens, close to works of art, were often inspired by paintings in the classical style of landscapes by Claude Lorraine and Nicolas Poussin. The work of Lancelot 'Capability' Brown, described as 'England's greatest gardener' was particularly influential. We hope that the reader is inspired by this book, and the long and varied history of gardening itself, to experiment with some home-gardening of their own. Enjoy.

Double Paeonies—New Varieties of Old-world Border Flowers

PREFACE

THE most satisfactory flowering plants for amateurs are hardy perennials—those which may be relied upon to provide a display in the open garden year after year. Fresh flowering stems appear in spring and die down in autumn, but the rootstocks live on and increase in size and vigour as the seasons pass; large clumps are formed which yield a profusion of blossom. Such plants are usually grouped together, with due regard to the colour of their flowers, and the result is seen in the Mixed Border, which is one of the most charming features of English gardens. A Mixed Border should be planted by everyone who has a garden, for it provides the maximum quantity of flowers at the minimum expenditure of time and labour. By making full use of various Annuals and Bulbs, and by planting with care and discrimination, it is possible to arrange a flower border that is attractive for the greater part of the summer and autumn months.

"Hardy Border Flowers" gives full directions upon such points of importance as Preparing the Ground, Planting, Arranging and Grouping, the Association of Colours, and so on, and contains a descriptive list of the most reliable flowers. The plans of flower borders have been prepared from sketches by Mr. F. W. Miles, who has also written the explanatory notes which accompany them.

H. H. T.

CONTENTS

CHAPTER	PAGE
1. The Mixed Flower Border	1
2. Planting Hardy Flowers	6
3. Arranging and Grouping	9
4. Hints on Cultivation and Manuring	13
5. Staking and Tying	16
6. Edging Plants	20
7. Grey Leaved Plants	23
8. Bulbs in the Flower Border	28
9. Biennials for the Border	33
10. Hardy Flowers from Seeds	36
11. Increasing Perennials by Division	40
12. Planting Perennials for Colour Effect	45
13. A Blue Flower Border	54
14. A White Flower Border	62
15. A Border of Mauve Flowers	69
16. A Pink and Rose Flower Border	74
17. A Border of Yellow Flowers	80
18. A Border of Red Flowers	87
19. A Border of Annual Flowers	94
20. Shrubs for the Flower Border	100
21. The Chief Hardy Border Flowers	104

ILLUSTRATIONS

	PAGE
Double Paeonies (Frontispiece)	1
Hardy flower borders	3
A garden of hardy flowers	5
Bold groups of Delphiniums	7
Groups of Dahlias and other autumn flowers	10
Three-year-old Chrysanthemum	11
Border of Phloxes	14
Anthemis tinctoria	17
Mossy Saxifrage as an edging	21
Perpetual flowering Pinks	25
King's Spear or Eremurus	29
The Martagon Lily	30
The Orange Lily	31
The Madonna Lily	32
Remarkable display of Snapdragons	34
Flowers of the Gaillardia	37
Old-world border flowers	38
The Shasta Daisy	39
Solomon's Seal	41
Vine-covered pillars and grassy ways	43
Late summer flowers	46
Peach-leaved Bellflower	47
Colour scheme for hardy flower border	49
Doronicum or Leopard's Bane	52
Blue flower border	56
Jacob's Ladder (Polemonium)	58
The Monkshood	60
White flower border	63
Flowers of Herbaceous Phlox	67

	PAGE
A mauve and purple corner	70
Mauve flower border	71
The Grecian Mallow	75
Pink and rose flower border	76
One of the Coneflowers	81
Yellow flower border	82
A handsome Torch Lily	85
Red flower border	88
Border Chrysanthemums	92
The best blue Sweet Pea	95
Candytuft, an indispensable annual	96
Border of annual flowers	97
Rhododendron in full bloom	101
A free-flowering Mock Orange	102
White Milfoil	105
The Japanese Anemone	107
Astilbe or Goat's Beard	108
The Carpathian Bellflower	110
Campanula, Telham Beauty	111
A dainty Bellflower	113
Border Carnations	115
Larkspur or annual Delphinium	117
Eryngium, or Sea Holly	119
Plantain Lily	120
A splendid border flower (Helenium)	121
A showy Sunflower	122
Cimicifuga racemosa	124
Bush Mallow (Lavatera)	127
A flower bed of Phlox	132
A handsome Mullein	138

HARDY BORDER FLOWERS

CHAPTER I

The Mixed Flower Border

A GARDEN border planted with a careful selection of hardy flowering plants is a source of interest and delight from spring until autumn. This form of gardening has become extremely popular in this country, especially during the present century, and that is scarcely surprising when one considers that it is in many ways the simplest of all, and while entailing the least labour and trouble, yet provides charming effects throughout the greater part of the years and yields innumerable flowers for cutting. In these way, it fulfils the expectations and satisfies the demands of the average grower and lover of flowers.

The mixed flower border is planted chiefly with hardy herbaceous perennials, though bulbs and annuals are also pressed into service. Occasionally, for the purpose of filling blanks left by the fading of early flowers, a few groups of tender, summer-flowering perennials are put in; and to prolong the gaiety of the border, Border Chrysanthemums, which have been grown in flower pots or in a reserve border, may be used. But even without the help of these additions it is possible to keep a mixed flower border reasonably gay from spring until autumn.

A hardy herbaceous perennial is a plant that is left undisturbed in the border from year to year without suffering harm, and makes fresh top growth annually from a perennial rootstock; the rootstock lives on for a varying number of years, while the flower stems develop and die within the year.

Annuals are plants which die after having flowered. If hardy, they may be sown in late summer out of doors in order to provide flowers in spring and early summer, but more commonly they are sown in spring to furnish flowers from July onwards.

Of bulbs, there are those that bloom in spring, summer and autumn, and the beauty of the hardy flower border may be extended very considerably by making use of some of them. As those that flower early are rather a nuisance when the blossoming season is past, owing to the untidiness of their leaves, their positions must be chosen with great care. They should be placed where, as far as is possible, their untidiness will be hidden by the advancing shoots or stems of later-flowering plants; there is no better place for them than among the clumps of such tall perennials as Michaelmas Daisies, Monkshoods, Heleniums, and others of that type. If they are so planted, their flowers may be enjoyed in the spring of the year, and as soon as the leaves begin to fade the vigorous shoots of the neighbouring perennials will hide them from view.

Equal care must be taken in placing the summer-flowering bulbs, especially those that remain undisturbed; otherwise they are certain to be damaged during times of renovation and cultivation. They should be set among plants that are best left alone for many years, such, for example, as Eryngium or Sea Holly, Gypsophila, Japanese Anemone, and so on.

In dealing with a large flower border it is well worth while considering whether a few flowering shrubs cannot be introduced with advantage. If the right sorts are chosen they are just as attractive when in bloom as the herbaceous perennials, and they possess this advantage over the latter, that they are of considerable decorative value even when out of bloom. Some of them are evergreen and are thus attractive all the year round; others may serve as a suitable setting for the brilliant flowers grouped round them; and all add a certain welcome stability of form and variety of outline to the border.

Hardy Flower Borders in a Welsh Garden

Certain climbing plants can often be used to great advantage in the mixed border, especially some of the rambling Roses and Clematis. When trained over tall poles at the back of the border they add immensely to its beauty during the summer season ; in spring, the fresh growths are pleasant to look upon, and even when the flowering season has passed, the lustrous green leaves which are typical of many rambling Roses certainly do not detract from the charm of the border.

A particularly happy way of making use of climbing Roses in the mixed flower border is by fixing posts at intervals of 10 to 12 feet and connecting them by means of chains or tarred rope, the latter being so arranged as to hang gracefully. The Roses soon reach the tops of the posts, and in the course of a season or two they will cover the hanging chains with festoons of leaf and blossom, which form a delightful background to the flower border. A similar series of posts and chains might well be arranged at the front of the border so that the display of flowers would be seen between garlands of Roses. It is better, especially at the front of the border, to connect the uprights with straight cross pieces of wood so that the view of the border is not obscured, and access to the plants for purposes of staking, tying, etc., is not hindered.

Although it cannot be gainsaid that the most imposing and satisfactory display is obtained from a wide and long border, that is not to say that a comparatively small border cannot be planted to produce a satisfactory result. The finest hardy flower borders are 15 feet or more in width, and 20 yards or more in length, but a very charming display throughout many months can be obtained from a border say 10 feet wide and 10 yards or more in length. The smaller the border the more carefully does it need to be planted, since blanks caused by plants which have gone out of bloom are more conspicuous. One has to be content with fewer plants of one kind.

In a large flower border it is usual to arrange the plants

THE MIXED FLOWER BORDER 5

in groups; this method gives a wonderful blaze of colour in the height of the summer season, and owing to the large numbers of other later-flowering plants near by, the dowdiness of those that have lost their beauty is not noticed, at all events in a general view of the border.

A Garden of Hardy Border Flowers

Biennials, of which the seed is sown one year to produce flowering plants the following year, such as Sweet William and Canterbury Bell, may be made use of, but in order to maintain a satisfactory display it is necessary to have a few Chrysanthemums to replace them; by the time the biennials are over it is then too late to sow seeds of annuals with any certainty of their proving satisfactory.

B

CHAPTER II

Planting Hardy Flowers

THE best time for planting most hardy herbaceous perennials is in October and November. They may also be put in during the winter months, and in spring as late as towards the end of March; but the later the planting is carried out, the less satisfactory will the plants prove to be the first summer. Some late flowering kinds such as Michaelmas Daisies and Monkshoods, together with a few that are liable to perish in winter in heavy land, as, for example, Gaillardia, Pyrethrum and Scabious, may be planted in spring, say late in February or early in March.

It is well worth while preparing the border thoroughly, for most of the plants must remain undisturbed for several years. Some are rather slow in becoming established, Gypsophila and Japanese Anemone, for instance, while others only reach their full beauty when they have had time to develop into large clumps; thus once planted they must not be interfered with, in some cases, for many years. I believe many gardeners, both amateur and professional, fail to get the best from some hardy herbaceous perennials because they persist in lifting and dividing them every few years, instead of leaving them undisturbed until such work is rendered essential by the deterioration of the plants.

The correct way to prepare a border for hardy flowers is to have it double dug or half trenched; in other words, it must be cultivated two spits or spade depths down. If the soil is heavy and clayey that means a good deal of hard work, but it pays handsomely. It is accomplished by first taking out a trench at one end of the border and wheeling

Bold Groups of Delphiniums and other Border Flowers

the excavated soil alongside the other end; the trench should be one spit deep and 18 inches or so wide. The bottom of the trench is then dug over, and manure, leaves, or garden refuse mixed with it. The adjoining top soil is then put in, thus filling the first trench and opening a second trench one spit deep.

The second trench is treated in a similar way, and the work proceeds until the whole of the border has been trenched; the soil first taken out is used to fill the last trench. Such materials as decayed manure, leaf-mould, wood ashes (and coal ashes if the soil is clayey), road scrapings, grit, sand, and old potting soil should be added to the surface soil and forked in, so as to render it as suitable as possible to the plants and to encourage the formation of roots.

A hole large enough to accommodate the roots of each plant should be taken out, and as the soil is filled in again it should be made fairly firm by treading. Care should be taken not to plant too deeply or there is a danger of the plants decaying during the wet, dull weather of winter. The crowns or centres of the plants should be arranged only just below the surface. If protection is thought to be necessary, though it is not required as a rule, it is best afforded by placing old ashes over the plants.

CHAPTER III

Arranging and Grouping

IT matters not how well grown are the plants, or how tidy is the border, if the arrangement of the border is faulty and the neighbouring colours are inharmonious the display will prove disappointing.

It is possible to have a beautiful and satisfactory flower border without creating elaborate colour schemes; in fact, the average amateur gardener will probably achieve better results if he concentrates upon avoiding colour discords than if he attempts to set out his border according to a prepared scheme in which the plants are grouped in colours.

The first things to consider are the comparative vigour and the heights of the plants made use of. Generally, the tallest will naturally be placed towards the back of the border, those of medium height in the middle, and the low growing kinds towards the front of the border. It is, however, a mistake to have a border of uniform outline; its appearance is far less interesting than when a taller plant or group of taller plants is allowed to encroach a little upon the lower kinds; similarly, the dwarf plants should be so disposed that here and there they run back into and between the tall plants.

Perhaps the greatest mistake of all is to use only one plant of a kind; they should be grouped at least three together, and if the extent of the border allows of it, five or even seven plants in each group will be better. So much depends upon the extent of ground at disposal. When the border is small, say not more than 9 or 10 feet wide and but a few yards long, the smaller plants should be in groups of three,

Groups of Dahlias, Michaelmas Daisies and other Autumn Flowers

ARRANGING AND GROUPING

while of the tall, vigorous kinds there will probably not be room for more than one or two of each.

An endeavour must be made to keep the groups of irregular

A Three-year-old Plant of Border Chrysanthemum

outline, and this will be found much easier of accomplishment if an odd number of plants is used rather than an even number. Even with three or five plants of one kind it is possible to arrange a border of very formal appearance, and that is exactly what one should try to avoid. If the outline of each group is in the form of an irregular circle, one plant being placed in the middle and the others at equal distances round it, the result will not be a happy one. An endeavour must be made to let one group run into the adjoining one ; some groups should extend sideways, others run towards the back of the border, and so on, each group being as irregular as possible and intermingling naturally and pleasingly with the others.

In the following pages plans and advice are given on the planting of flower borders of one colour for those who wish and have the opportunity of creating borders of this kind, and there are plans showing how to plant a border of various colours with due regard to the correct grouping of the latter. If it is found impossible to carry out the latter in its entirety, some of the colours which are shown to commingle harmoniously may be used in a smaller border. For example, a blue and white border is very beautiful, or one of blue and yellow flowers is very handsome, while pink and light blue, pale yellow and pale blue are examples of other colours which may be grouped with excellent effect.

In planting a large border for colour effect it is best to begin with white flowers, and gradually to work up to red through pale blue, blue, pink, and rose, keeping the brilliant reds and orange shades to the middle of the border. The second part of the border should be arranged in a similar fashion so that the colours gradually fade from red through orange to yellow, blue, rose, and lavender to white.

CHAPTER IV

Hints on Cultivation and Manuring

PROVIDING the border was prepared for planting in the way described, the plants will need little further attention in matters of cultivation and manuring for the first year or two. Subsequently, however, steps must be taken to keep the soil fertile and the roots supplied with plant foods in adequate quantity. Nothing does so much good as an application of stable or farmyard manure in a partially decayed state. This not only supplies the plants with nourishment, but it provides the ground with humus, and that is one of the chief essentials of garden soil. Such material is, however, often difficult to obtain nowadays, and always expensive, and it may be necessary to provide substitutes. Leaf-mould is excellent to apply as a top-dressing to flower borders in spring, while spent hops, road scrapings, pieces of turf, soil in which pot plants have been grown, and wood ashes are all excellent, and compensate, in part at least, for the absence of yard or stable manure. On heavy land sifted ashes may be applied in winter with advantage, for they render the soil more workable and assist its drainage. Leaves should be gathered in autumn and made into heaps; by spring they will be sufficiently decayed for putting on the border.

The best time to apply manure is in early spring, as soon as the border has been forked over and tidied up for the season. If put on in autumn or winter the manure keeps the ground cold and wet, and prevents its exposure to air, frost and snow, which is so beneficial. Further, if heaped closely round the dormant plants, manure harbours soil

A Border of Herbaceous Phloxes

CULTIVATION AND MANURING

pests, and may result in the decay of some of the less hardy kinds.

It is useless to apply artificial manures to a flower border of which the soil is deficient in humus or decayed vegetable matter, which is supplied by yard manure, leaf-mould, and so on. They must not be regarded as substitutes for these, but rather as additions to them. The best general artificial manure for the flower border is basic slag; this ought to be applied in early autumn at the rate of about 6 oz. to the square yard. If this is supplemented by superphosphate of lime, at the rate of 2 oz. per square yard in spring, the plants are not likely to suffer from a lack of phosphates, which are so essential to the production of a satisfactory harvest of blossom.

Sulphate of ammonia and nitrate of soda are quick acting artificial manures, which are useful for application in spring to assist the growth of backward plants, but, as a rule, they are not required so far as border plants are concerned.

In late February or early in March, as soon as the soil is reasonably dry, the border should be carefully forked over to loosen the soil, which is certain to have been made somewhat sodden by the winter rains. After having been turned over to the depth of 3 or 4 inches with the garden fork, it will soon be in a condition when it may be further broken down by means of the Dutch hoe. From spring until late summer the hoe should be used frequently, at least once a week; this invaluable garden tool destroys weeds, both large and small, especially if used in hot, dry weather, and keeps the surface soil loose, thus preventing the evaporation of moisture.

CHAPTER V

Staking and Tying

As the spring merges into summer the border plants make rapid progress, and many of them must be adequately supported, or the stems will fall over and become bent and misshapen ; if that should happen it is almost impossible again to get them perpendicular, and the appearance of the border will be spoilt. Although some artificial support is undoubtedly required, especially by the vigorous plants, it should be as unobtrusive as possible, otherwise the remedy may be worse than the evil.

Amateurs rarely support their plants properly and well. Either they make use of bulky sticks, which are far too conspicuous, or they do not support the plants early enough. Some there are who insert one strong stake, bunch all the flower stems together, and tie them to the stake, thus destroying all the charm and grace of the plants and their flower display.

The chief points to bear in mind are to use as few sticks or stakes as possible, to choose them of such a height that when the plants are in full bloom the sticks will be hidden by the stems and shoots, and to see that staking is done early in the season, before the growths have grown so high that they are unable to support themselves.

The best supports for many slender growing plants of moderate height are pea sticks thrust among the developing shoots ; they are sufficiently strong to keep these upright, yet when the plants are full grown they are seen scarcely, if at all, and do not in the least detract from the natural grace and beauty of the plants ; they do in fact add greatly

STAKING AND TYING

to the value of the display because they ensure that the flower stems are held well up to view.

When dealing with vigorous kinds, such as Delphinium, which have comparatively few strong stems that are partially self-supporting, it is sometimes sufficient to use bands of string at about 12 inches apart, from a height of 2 feet or so from the ground to a height of 4 or 5 feet. More often,

A Hardy Yellow Flower for the Border, Anthemis tinctoria

however, it is essential to have three stakes inserted towards the outside of the clump round which the string can be twisted, thus strengthening the support. The sticks can be placed behind some of the stems, and as the string bands will not be visible from a short distance, such support, while adequate, is not noticeable, and is therefore ideal.

When staking vigorous perennials which produce numerous flowering stems, such as Helenium and Michaelmas Daisy, it is best to insert a number of strong sticks near the base of the plant, and to incline them outwards, so that the heads of flower when in full beauty will not be crowded together, yet are prevented from being blown about and damaged by wet and windy weather. Bands of tarred string passed round the sticks from half way up the latter to near their tops will finish off the work satisfactorily.

Groups of annuals may usually be given sufficient support by placing twiggy pea sticks among them, or by placing sticks round the outside of the groups and connecting them by string or raffia. The way to stake Dahlias is to drive in one stout stake and to attach the shoots loosely to this by means of raffia. In all cases, the raffia or other tying material should first be passed round the stake so that it will not slip; it is then a good plan to twist the strands several times before they are fastened round the flower stems. Raffia is a far cheaper material for tying than string, and if it is twisted instead of being used in its natural flat state its strength is increased, and it is less conspicuous. Raffia is much easier to handle if it is first well moistened.

Cutting down Perennials in Autumn.—Inquiries are often made concerning the work of cutting down the stems of herbaceous perennials in autumn. This is a matter that needs some consideration. Why, for instance, should not some of them be allowed to remain for the sake of their decorative appearance throughout the autumn and early winter months? It is true that there may be some disadvantage in allowing the plants to bear such large numbers of seeds as will naturally result if the flower stems are not interfered with, but at least, so far as the vigorous perennials are concerned, that does not appear to have any deleterious effect upon their welfare. How decorative, for example, are the old flower stems of Spiraea, Astilbe, Michaelmas Daisy, Japanese Stonecrop, and others! It is true that they are somewhat untidy, and those who have a passion for neatness in the garden are not likely to let them remain,

CUTTING DOWN PERENNIALS

once their beauty is past. But in the depth of winter they do relieve the monotonous aspect of the hardy flower border, and are at least pleasanter to look upon than the bare soil.

While some herbaceous perennials are wholly deciduous—losing all their leaves at the approach of autumn—others have evergreen leaves, though their flower stems die down. Those belonging to the former class may be cut off almost to the ground level in late autumn, if it is wished to have the border thoroughly tidy for the winter. On the other hand, those possessing evergreen leaves and deciduous flower stems must not be interfered with except that the latter may be cut off. Take the Flag Irises and Torch Lilies (Tritoma) for example; it would be incorrect and damaging to interfere with the green leaves; in the case of the Torch Lilies, which are liable to suffer damage from frosts, the leaves afford valuable protection in winter; in spring all that are dead or disfigured should be cut off.

CHAPTER VI

Edging Plants

THE selection of plants used in forming a margin to the hardy flower border is of importance, for the appearance of the display is easily marred by an injudicious choice, as it is enhanced by a judicious choice. If the border is next to a lawn care should be taken that the edging plants do not encroach on the grass, otherwise this is liable to be disfigured or even destroyed. If a gravel walk runs alongside the border, an opportunity arises of making an edging of rough stones, such as the smaller pieces of sandstone used in building a rockery; or bricks may be used, though they should not be so arranged that they form a serrated line, as is sometimes seen. An edging of that kind is only a degree better than one of flints stuck on end and limewashed or painted white—easily the worst form of edging that has ever been thought of.

A flower border never looks better than when it runs alongside a flagged or paved path; the edging plants may then encroach on the path as they will, and in doing so they form a natural and altogether delightful margin to the border, caressing the cool stones with warm masses of colour or flinging their trailing flower-studded growths over them.

Edging plants ought not, I think, to be planted in a long straight line, although it is true that such a line of white Pinks bordering a long border is very charming in June. But such a plan accentuates the hard line of the margin, and it should be the aim of the planter to merge the groups into each other naturally so that no hard, straight lines are seen. Edging plants should be grouped just as

EDGING PLANTS

One of the Loveliest of Edging Plants, Mossy Saxifrage

those in other parts of the border are grouped; as they are smaller more of them will be needed in each group. When thus arranged they are more attractive than when disposed in a straight line.

When the flower border runs alongside the lawn such plants should be chosen as are not likely to encroach, or that can be trimmed to keep them from spreading on the grass. Such are suitable as Thrift, Violas, Pinks, Heuchera, London Pride, Perennial Candytuft, the yellow Alyssum saxatile, the grey-leaved Stachys lanata, and Veronica incana, a plant of low growth having greyish leaves and blue flowers.

When the border runs by a gravel or paved walk one may choose plants that look best when they are allowed to trail over the margin, forming hummocky tufts here and spreading into slender trails there; for example, Silvery Saxifrages, Woolly Thyme (Thymus lanuginosus), Mossy Saxifrages, Campanula rupestris (a dainty and free flowering dwarf Bellflower), Nepeta Mussinii, the Helianthemum or Sun Rose, and Snow in Summer (Cerastium tomentosum).

CHAPTER VII

Grey-leaved Plants

EVERY flower border ought to contain a few grey-leaved or silver-leaved plants; they are attractive throughout the year and particularly interesting in winter. It is very desirable to place the grey-leaved plants in a sunny position. In shady positions and cramped surroundings most of them lack the glistening silvery character which is so striking when the plants are grown in the open garden.

The kind of soil in which they are planted influences the quality of leaf colour. In any soil the leaves will naturally have a greyish appearance, but the best results are only secured in well-drained ground which has been tilled and manured. For some plants in particular, notably Wormwood and Lavender, a warm, light soil is desirable.

Most grey-leaved plants flower freely and produce seeds which allow of their being increased without difficulty. Taking cuttings and dividing the clumps also provide means of propagating most of the plants named.

Achillea (Milfoil or Yarrow).—The Yarrows thrive in ordinary soil in sunny positions, flower in summer, and are best increased by division in late autumn and early winter. Those with grey or silver foliage are: argentea, snow white, 4 inches; Huteri, white, 6 inches; Kellererii, white, 6 inches; and umbellata vera, white, 6 inches.

Alyssum (Rock Madwort).—These thrive in any well-drained soil, and should be planted in a sunny position. Cuttings in late summer and division in early autumn are the usual methods of increase, though they are also readily raised from seeds sown in April or May. The chief sorts are : rostratum, golden-yellow, 9 inches ; saxatile, golden yellow, 12 inches, very showy in masses ; spinosum, white 4 inches. All flower in spring.

Antennaria tomentosa.—This forms a perfect carpet of grey foliage, and in spring and early summer the masses of white flowers, 4 or 5 inches high, are well described by its popular name. Increase is by division, cuttings and seeds.

Artemisia Abrotanum (Southernwood or Old Man). —Has finely-cut, greyish or hoary foliage, and grows 2 to 4 feet high. Prune in March. Others are : argentea (Silvery Wormwood), silvery-white foliage, $1\frac{1}{2}$ feet ; stelleriana, a creeping Wormwood, with silvery foliage, 6 inches. Plant in ordinary light soil and a sunny position. Increase by cuttings in August.

Cerastium tomentosum.—Silvery-white foliage, white flowers in early summer, 4 to 6 inches high. This plant makes a good permanent edging. It is readily increased by seeds, cuttings and division, and should be cut well back after flowering.

Dianthus caesius (Cheddar Pink).—This is excellent for an edging and for planting between the crevices of a paved walk. It is 4 inches high, and has rosy-pink fragrant blossoms in summer. Mix plenty of old mortar rubble with the soil before planting. Border Pinks must be included among the grey-leaved plants. The following twelve sorts are easy to grow, and have fragrant flowers : Albino, white ; Anne Boleyn, deep pink, crimson centre ; Diamond, white ; Early Blush, pink ; Early Red, rose, crimson centre ; Elsie, deep rose ; fimbriatus alba major, white ; Gloriosa, rosy mauve ; Her Majesty, white ; Mrs. Sinkins, white ; Paddington, red, plum - coloured centre, and Rose de Mai, cerise pink. Pinks are increased by division of the clumps during September and October.

Helianthemum (Sun Rose).—For planting towards the front of the border or for covering sunny banks, the

GREY-LEAVED PLANTS

Sun Roses are valuable dwarf evergreen shrubs, 4 to 6 inches high. They flower very freely from May to July, and are readily increased by cuttings inserted in a cold frame or handlight during August and September. Three sorts

Flowers of Dianthus Allwoodii, or Perpetual-flowering Pinks

with silver-grey leaves are : Beauty, rose pink ; Mrs. Croft, rose ; and The Bride, pure white.

Lavandula (Lavender).—The Munstead Early Dwarf Lavender has earlier and darker flowers than the common kind on bushes not more than 1 foot high ; the Dutch variety is also more " bushy," and has lighter grey leaves, hence is more effective. Lavender bushes are kept neat and trim by clipping after flowering. Cuttings root readily under a handlight in late summer.

Lychnis coronaria (Crown Campion)—Another name for this favourite rose red flower is Agrostemma coronaria. It grows 2 to 3 feet high, flowering throughout the summer. At other times the plants are a mass of hoary grey leaves. This is one of the few grey-leaved plants which really do well in partial shade. There is a white-flowered sort, and atrosanguinea has deep rose-crimson blooms. Self-sown seedlings are frequent, and the plants may be increased by division.

Nepeta Mussinii.—This is one of our best dwarf border flowers, 12 to 18 inches high. From May to September the grey leaves are almost hidden by masses of lavender blue blossoms. Increase is by division of the clumps in October or March, and by cuttings.

Salvia argentea is the Silvery Clary; it has hoary or silvery, woolly foliage and white flowers, 3 feet. The Common Sage, Salvia pratensis, is an attractive grey bush some 2 to 3 feet high. Increase is easy by seeds, cuttings and division.

Saxifraga (Rockfoil).—The free use of the encrusted Silver Saxifragas will add considerable interest to the flower border margin. The plants form silvery rosette-like tufts about 2 inches high. They like well drained, gritty soil containing lime, and are readily increased by division. Special mention may be made of cochlearis, crustata, lingulata superba, longifolia and Rocheliana.

Scabiosa pterocephala.—This is one of the dwarf Pincushion Flowers with spreading tufts of grey foliage which make a useful permanent edging; it grows about 6 inches high. In summer and autumn the mauve-purple blossoms are showy. Increase is by division in October or March.

Sedum (Stonecrop).—S. Ewersii is a distinct and useful plant with grey-green foliage, 4 inches high, with rose-coloured flowers in summer. Sedum glaucum is a very small plant that forms a grey cushion, and makes a neat, permanent edging. S. spathulifolium is dwarf and spreading in habit, with yellow flowers in June. All are readily increased by division and thrive in ordinary soil.

Stachys lanata (Lamb's Tongue).—This is one of the best grey edging plants with silvery white, woolly leaves. It is easy to grow and increase is by division.

Thymus (Thyme).—The Silver Lemon Thyme (Thymus citriodorus argenteus) grows about 9 inches high, and has silver-variegated scented leaves. Increase is by cuttings and division.

Veronica incana (Grey Speedwell).—This grows 6 inches high, the silvery grey foliage being very attractive in winter. From June to August the violet-blue flowers are attractive.

CHAPTER VIII

Bulbs in the Flower Border

BULBS are apt to be rather a nuisance in the mixed flower border because, to some extent, they prevent the proper cultivation of the soil between the plants, and unless great care is taken, and their positions are accurately known, many of them are bound to be damaged during the work of cultivation and when alterations and re-arrangements are undertaken. Nevertheless, they are so useful, and those that bloom in spring so valuable because they flower when the border plants have scarcely begun to make fresh growth, that an endeavour should be made to include a selection of them. So far as the spring flowering kinds are concerned, and particularly the Daffodils, I find it is best to plant a few groups among the vigorous perennials towards the back of the border; they will be appreciated in March and April, and as the perennials start to grow their fading leaves will soon be hidden. One can always manage to put in a few clumps in such positions, and in other odd corners where they are not likely to be in the way or to be disturbed.

So far as summer flowering bulbs are concerned one must arrange for their inclusion and take careful note of their positions, for they should be looked upon as indispensable. Among these are Spanish and English Irises in brilliant colours; they ought to be planted in October. The Spanish Irises are obtainable in shades of blue and yellow; they grow about 20 inches high, and should be planted at 3 inches apart and at about the same depth. English Irises in shades of purple and mauve, chiefly, are more vigorous, reaching a height of 2 feet or so; the bulbs should be about

King's Spear, or Eremurus

6 inches apart and some 4 inches deep. The tuberous roots of the inimitable blue-flowered Salvia patens ought to be

started into growth in the greenhouse in spring, and planted out of doors in May.

There are many delightful Lilies suitable for planting in the mixed flower border. The chief favourite is the Madonna Lily (Lilium candidum), which bears its exquisite spires of white blooms in June : the bulbs ought to be planted in August or early in September, so that they will produce a

The Martagon Lily (Lilium Martagon)

strong tuft of leaves before winter. If planted later they are not likely to bloom the following year. This lovely white Lily associates charmingly with the blue-flowered Delphiniums or Larkspurs, and should, if possible, be planted near them.

Another valuable Lily for the mixed border is the Japanese Lilium speciosum, which bears large, handsome flowers, white, marked and spotted with rose or crimson, in late

BULBS IN THE FLOWER BORDER

summer and autumn. This, and the Madonna Lily, thrive in ordinary loamy soil, and increase in size and beauty from year to year.

Lilium croceum, the old Orange Lily, is very showy when its large and brilliant orange red blooms are in full beauty in June, and thrives without any special care. Lilium Thunbergianum and Lilium elegans are two other good

The Orange Lily (Lilium croceum)

Lilies suitable for planting near the front of the border; they bloom in June, and the colour of the flowers is some shade of yellow or orange. The Panther Lily (Lilium pardalinum) is a tall and particularly handsome flower, crimson with orange spots; it thrives best in partial shade, and the site for it should be prepared by adding peat, leaf-mould and sand. Lilium Henryi, a tall pale orange-flowered Lily, and Lilium testaceum (the Nankeen Lily), with nankeen yellow blossoms, and Lilium regale, are other good Lilies for the flower border.

Gladioli, which are now obtainable in innumerable shades of colour, are invaluable for providing flowers from late July until the end of August if a representative selection is chosen. The roots are planted towards the end of March in well-prepared ground with which some sand, leaf-mould

The Lovely Old White Madonna Lily that blooms in June

and wood ashes have been mixed; they should be placed 2 to 3 inches deep. The old scarlet-flowered Gladiolus Brenchleyensis is still worth growing, but it is surpassed in beauty by many of the modern kinds.

The Cape Hyacinth (Galtonia candicans) bears drooping, bell-shaped white flowers on stems 3 feet or so high in August, and is invaluable. The bulbs are taken up in autumn and are replanted in March. Eremurus, illustrated on page 29, is very handsome. The roots should be planted in early autumn.

CHAPTER IX

Biennials for the Border

AMONG the biennials are such favourite flowers as Sweet William, Canterbury Bell, Wallflower, Polyanthus, Aquilegia, Foxglove, the tall and handsome Chimney Bellflower (Campanula pyramidalis), and Honesty. Some of these are really perennials, but they are best treated as biennials, either because they are not reliable after the first flowering or because freshly raised plants make a better show. Most of the biennials will be found useful at various seasons of the year for adding colour to the display. They may be grouped among some of the latest flowering perennials, and will serve to brighten up those portions of the border which otherwise might remain somewhat dull until the permanent plants come into flower. If they are taken up immediately the blossoms have faded they will not interfere with the development of the permanent plants. Such as Wallflower and Polyanthus are very attractive in spring before many of the chief plants have commenced to bloom, while Aquilegia or Columbine is so beautiful, if the modern long spurred varieties are grown, that room ought certainly to be found for them. In some soils they may be left undisturbed, but as a rule it is more satisfactory to raise them afresh from seed each year. Foxgloves are picturesque when planted among the coarser perennials at the back of the border, and once a few plants have been grown there will always be enough self-sown seedlings for replanting. They should be taken up in early autumn and planted out where they are to bloom the following year. The white Foxglove is a charming flower, far surpassing in beauty

A Remarkable Display of Snapdragons

BIENNIALS

those of reddish purple colouring. Sweet Williams and Canterbury Bells are invaluable, for their display lasts for many weeks if care is taken to prevent the formation of seed by removing the faded flowers. Such as these, which continue to bloom well into the summer, should be replaced by Border Chrysanthemums.

Seeds of the biennials should be sown in May so that strong plants may be available for planting out in autumn. If sowing is delayed until July the seedlings do not have the same opportunity of making progress. In growing the giant Chimney Bellflower (Campanula pyramidalis), which produces handsome spires of blue flowers 4 to 5 feet high, seed should be sown under glass, in frame or greenhouse, in March, otherwise it is doubtful if the plants will bloom the following year.

With this exception the seed of biennials is sown in May in boxes of finely sifted soil, placed in a frame, which should be kept closed until the seeds germinate. The seed boxes must be covered with pieces of glass to keep the soil uniformly moist. When the seedlings are of such a size that they can be handled conveniently, they are transplanted at greater distances apart in other boxes, and in a month or two will be large enough to be put out of doors on a reserve border; there they will remain until they can be planted permanently in autumn.

CHAPTER X

Hardy Flowers from Seeds

IT is so easy to raise most hardy border flowers from seed that it is a matter for surprise so few amateurs attempt to provide a stock of plants in this way.

The best time to sow is in April and May. Some of the larger seeds, such as those of Lupin, may be sown out of doors in well-prepared soil brought to a fine tilth, but it is better to sow all seeds of border perennials in boxes of fine soil placed in a frame. If the frame is kept closed, and the soil moist by syringeing, the seeds of most kinds germinate in a few weeks, and the seedlings, if carefully tended, will develop into quite good plants by autumn and will flower the following year. Some, of course, take longer to make strong plants than others, but the majority can be relied upon to be large enough for permanent planting in autumn or spring. When the seedlings are first seen, the pieces of glass which were placed on the boxes to help to keep the soil uniformly moist should be removed, so that the little plants may have more air and light. They must be watered very carefully while small or they are liable to damp off. It is better to moisten them by means of the syringe while they remain in the box in which the seeds were sown. They must be shaded from sunshine also. As soon as the little plants are of such a size that they can be handled conveniently, say an inch high or rather less, they should be transplanted singly to small flower-pots of soil, or into other boxes in which they will be placed at a greater distance apart, say 2 inches. There they may remain for about two months, when most of them will be large enough

The Gay Gaillardia—the Blooms are chiefly Red and Yellow.
Easily raised from seed

to plant out on a reserve border preferably in partial shade. Some will be large enough to be planted in the border in autumn, and others in spring.

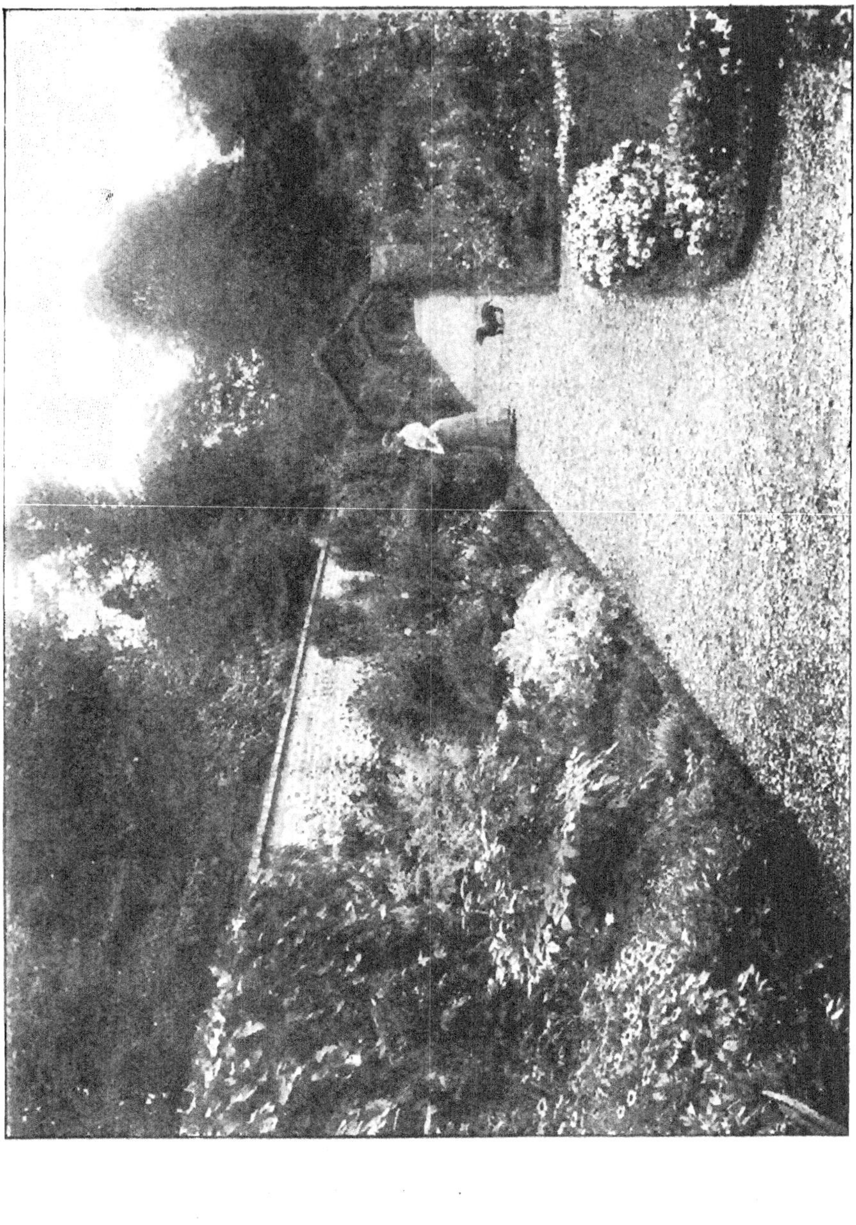

HARDY FLOWERS FROM SEEDS

It is astonishing in how short a time one may raise large numbers of hardy border plants in this way, and they have the advantage over those raised from cuttings and by division that they are generally more vigorous and longer lived.

Some hardy border flowers that are very easily raised in this way are Oriental Poppy, Lupin, Delphinium, Geum,

The Shasta Daisy (Chrysanthemum maximum)

Potentilla, Campanula, Carnation, Pink, Valerian, Monkshood, Shasta Daisy, or Hardy Marguerite, Viola, Pansy, Linum or Flax, Aquilegia, Achillea, Pyrethrum, Hollyhock, and Border Chrysanthemum. Such as Lupin, Poppy, Geum, Potentilla, Valerian, Achillea, Carnation, and Pink make an excellent display in one year from seed. Such as Viola, Pansy, Hollyhock, and Aquilegia are best treated as annuals.

CHAPTER XI

Increasing Perennials by Division

THE propagation of hardy border perennials by division of the clumps or roots is the most generally practised means of increasing the stock. This method is practised because it is simple and requires no greenhouse or frame, and the new plants are facsimiles of the old ones, whereas seedlings may vary little or much in colour of flower and growth. Further, the flowering of the plants is little affected, unless the clumps are divided into very small portions.

In a garden with a representative collection of herbaceous perennials, the increase of the plants by division is practically continuous throughout the year. Most of the work is done when the weather is mild and the ground not too wet, between October and March. A useful general rule to follow is to divide spring and early summer flowers during the autumn and early winter. We may take as examples Lupins, Oriental Poppies, Aquilegias, and Doronicums. Plants which flower from August to November may be propagated in late winter and early spring. These include Michaelmas Daisies, Border Chrysanthemums, Sedum spectabile and Perennial Sunflowers.

' After the lifting, dividing, and replanting, the roots will be practically lifeless for some time. It would not harm such plants as Michaelmas Daisies, for instance, to take them up in mid-winter, but the Dropmore Alkanet and Lupins, for example, might be damaged, and might fail to start into growth in spring. If these are divided and replanted during October, or September, when the ground is warm and the weather mild, they make new roots,

INCREASING PERENNIALS

Solomon's Seal, one of the most satisfactory of all hardy plants. Thrives on a shady border

and become established in the new place before winter. Similarly, in early spring, if the propagation of important plants is done towards the end of February and during

March, the weather and ground conditions are rapidly improving, with the result that they commence growth at once. The Japanese Anemone, in particular, should not be disturbed until March is well advanced : as it blooms until late in the autumn it cannot be lifted then.

Other things, however, being favourable, choose October and November in preference to the spring for the majority of plants, and for this reason. When a dry spring or summer follows early spring planting, considerable watering will be necessary, and even then the plants seldom make such good growth as those moved in autumn, for the latter are well established by April or May. In heavy soils, dividing and replanting is frequently done in March. Sometimes it is thought worth while to lift the clumps in November and store them away safely in a sheltered corner in light soil until spring. This gives an opportunity of cultivating the ground in winter and of leaving the soil exposed to the action of the weather.

Dealing with plants which it is desirable to divide between March and September it will suffice to name a few notable examples. April is the best month to transplant the large clumps of the Torch Lily (Kniphofia). During May it is usual to divide and replant Violets. In June and July popular spring-flowering plants are propagated ; notable examples are Primrose, Polyanthus, Double Daisies, Spring Saxifrages, Arabis, Aubrietia, and Perennial Candytuft. August is the month to divide the Madonna Lily (Lilium candidum), and in September Pansies, Violas, and Pinks should be lifted, divided and replanted.

While some kinds appear to be indifferent to rough treatment, a clump of Michaelmas Daisies or Helenium may be chopped into four or five pieces with a spade for example, others require careful handling. In dealing with small clumps use two handforks, thrust in back to back, and force the handles away from each other. With large clumps, the herbaceous Phlox, for example, two ordinary digging

Vine-covered Pillars and Grassy Ways in the Flower Garden

Photo: F. Mason Good

forks may be similarly employed with satisfactory results. The number of pieces into which a clump may be safely parted is a point worthy of consideration. It is not desirable to split up a clump of Delphiniums into more than two, three or four pieces. On the other hand, quite small pieces of the Michaelmas Daisy are satisfactory; one fair size clump may yield, perhaps, a dozen pieces if this number is required. In nurseries, where large numbers of plants are needed, the clumps are frequently divided up into single "crowns," each with a few roots attached. While the best of the pieces may be planted directly in the border, to ensure every piece growing they are usually potted and placed in a cold frame for two months or so.

When the stock of plants is abundant always select the pieces on the outside of the clumps for replanting. These are always the best. If, in replanting a border, the clumps are lifted and have to remain out of the ground for several days, place leaves round them, covering them with a mat as a protection from frost. It should be hardly necessary to emphasize the importance of labelling the clumps plainly before lifting.

CHAPTER XII

Planting Perennials for Colour Effect

IF a new herbaceous border is to be made, or an old one lifted and rearranged, the first thing demanding attention is the soil. Unless perennials have a good and moderately rich soil, growth of many plants will be stunted and the flowers will not be up to standard either in size or in colour. The site should be double-dug and enriched by liberal application of organic manure before the plants are placed in position, in the way described on page 6. On light soils the planting of perennials may be carried out at almost any time, except in frosty weather, during the autumn and winter.

Many herbaceous borders are spoilt because of the straight line along the front of them. A perfectly straight border may be desirable when the whole is to assume imposing proportions, or when two borders run along the sides of a straight wide path. Many readers, however, have not so much space to spare, and they make their borders look larger by planning in such a way that the outline is irregular. A suitable background is important. An Ivy-clad wall provides an ideal background, but only in rare cases is there a wall. Certainly more use might be made of Pillar Roses as a background; varieties such as Shower of Gold, Hiawatha, Minnehaha and Blush Rambler are ideal.

A beautiful setting can be provided for herbaceous plants by planting a row of Sweet Peas along the back. Between Roses and Sweet Peas the reader must make a choice, or both may be used with charming effect if care is taken to select varieties suitable in colour for that section of the border in which they are to be planted.

Late Summer Flowers—Japanese Anemones are seen in the background, Stocks and Japanese Stonecrop in front

PLANTING FOR COLOUR EFFECT 47

The foreground is no less important than the background. When the border runs alongside a gravel path a low stone edging might be provided over which suitable plants could trail. A grass path forms, perhaps, the most restful setting for a hardy flower border, and if this is available somewhat taller edging plants may be used and the stones will not be necessary.

To display the varying colours effectively the border must be fairly wide and groups of fair size planted. The

A Splendid Border Flower : Double-white Peach-leaved Bell-flower (Campanula Moerheimi)

average amateur employs too many plants, with the result that a patchwork quilt effect is produced. True, gorgeous displays of colour may often be noted in the amateur's herbaceous border, but indiscriminate association of colours brings about crude contrasts. The intelligent worker will so arrange the plants that harmony is more in evidence than glaring contrasts. He will endeavour also to group the plants so that three or five of each sort will stand together. Hardy border flowers should be so arranged that, when in bloom, a restful, old-world appearance may result. The only way to achieve this is by blending the yellows purples, whites, pinks, blues and rose shades properly. The more brilliant colours, such as the crimsons, scarlets and reds, should not be employed too freely, and in any case their colours must be subdued to some extent by planting flowers with softer tones around them.

The varying shades of blue associate charmingly with soft yellows. Rose and pink shades may also be merged into the stronger yellows with effect, but the scarlet and crimson flowers must be kept away from the blues and yellows. Break up these warm colours with a foil of white flowers, while, when the white section is being planted, a number of silvery-grey foliage plants should be introduced between them to avoid all possibility of a hard white effect being obtained.

Naturally one wants the hardy flower border to be attractive for as long as possible. This period may be prolonged if the planter associates certain spring-flowering plants, annuals, and biennials with the choicer perennials. For example, spaces should always be left along the front of the herbaceous border for the introduction of dwarf Anemones and bulbs, such as Narcissi and May-flowering Tulips. Wallflowers, too, might well be pressed into service for spring displays, following these with Snapdragons, Ostrich Plume Asters, or whatever were fancied during the summer. Spaces should be left for Sweet Williams and Canterbury Bells, and Pentstemons are also useful.

Thus it will be seen that such plants as Alyssum, Arabis, Doronicum, Daffodil, Tulip, Wallflower, etc., may enliven the border during spring, and plants of Gaillardia and Paeony continue the display in early summer. For the months of June, July, and August there is such a wealth of bloom available that one need not particularize except to lay stress on the point that free use should be made of Delphinium, Phlox, Madonna Lilies and Anchusa. The border will be no less beautiful in autumn if a good selection of Michaelmas Daisies is planted and Rudbeckias are made sufficient use

Colour Scheme for Hardy Flower Border—First Part

White flowers with Silvery-grey Foliage Plants — *Rose & Pink shades*

- Spiræa Aruncus
- Bocconia cordata
- Pillar Rose White Dorothy
- Aster White Climax
- Lupinus Snow Queen
- Astilbe rivularis
- Hollyhock Lady Bailey
- Pillar Rose Lady Gay
- Spiræa venusta
- Salvia argentea
- Aster Albatross
- Madonna Lilies
- Astilbe thunbergi
- Phlox Niphetos
- Phlox Sheriff Ivory
- Aster Lil Fardell
- Astilbe Davidii
- Chrysanthemum K. Edward VII
- Pyrethrum Princess Irene
- Cimicifuga racemosa
- Sweet William Pink Beauty
- Canterbury Bells Pink
- Pyrethrum Pink Pearl
- Cerastium tomentosum
- Allwoodii Harold
- Viola Virgin White
- Carnation Raby Castle
- Pentstemon James Douglas
- Allwoodii Rufus

Colour Scheme for Hardy Flower Border—Second Part

Colour Scheme for Hardy Flower Border—Third Part

Doronicum, or Leopard's Bane, is one of the best plants for shaded places; the yellow flowers are borne freely in April

PLANTING FOR COLOUR EFFECT

of. Dahlias, Border Chrysanthemums, Heleniums, Golden Rods and perennial Sunflowers are also indispensable.

Apart from securing the proper colour blends in a border of hardy flowers, the grouping of the plants with due regard to their heights is important. Too often the amateur is absurdly slavish in his adherence to the principle of placing tall plants at the back, and working them down until he arrives at the dwarfs in front. It is a mistake to put such a plan into detailed practice. The result obtained is very formal and the plants are very like soldiers on parade. By placing an occasional group of tall plants towards the front of the border, the general outline will be relieved and the note of strict formality avoided. Choose fairly tall plants with pretty foliage for this grouping. The one-cclour border is capable of producing results quite arresting in their beauty, and this side of flower gardening is dealt with in succeeding chapters.

E

CHAPTER XIII

A Blue Flower Border

A BLUE border shows perhaps to greatest advantage when backed by a grey wall on which Clematises, such as Beauty of Worcester and Lady Northcliffe, or Wistaria sinensis, are grown. Better even than these would be the beautiful Ceanothus Brilliant, with dark green foliage and rich blue flowers. This climber is very attractive in early summer and autumn, and is really one of the best wall plants available. A close study of the plans illustrating this chapter will show that the blue flower border is attractive in the summer, autumn and the early spring months.

Blue spring-flowering plants are not numerous, but those available are very good and a fine display may be obtained by making full use of them. Among bulbous plants are the charming Chionodoxas, the feathery Grape Hyacinths and Scillas, whilst the Forget-me-nots should be made full use of. There is no reason why the many spaces allotted to annual flowers in the front of the border should not be bedded with Forget-me-nots in the autumn. A groundwork of these flowers might even be spread round the various perennials farther back in the border. There are two excellent varieties in Royal Blue and Perfection. The former has long sprays of deep indigo-blue flowers, while Perfection is of lighter hue and dwarfer in habit. Then in late spring Violas such as Blue Diamond and True Blue will prove attractive, and use might be made of Blue Primroses.

The chief plants in a blue border in the height of summer must be Delphiniums, and it is difficult to think of any other plant which combines stateliness with beauty in such a way.

Blue Flower Border—First Part

Blue Flower Border—Second Part

Blue Flower Border—Third Part

All the varieties marked on the plan are good. Rev. E. Lascelles, 5 feet, is a striking royal blue ; Queen Wilhelmina, 4 feet, has beautiful pale blue single flowers ; Persimmon is similar, but not quite so tall ; and Perfection, 5 feet, is another light blue, with flowers produced on massive spikes ;

Jacob's Ladder (Polemonium coeruleum), a blue-flowered hardy plant

Col. Douglas, 6 feet, is a striking rich blue ; Mrs. Thompson, 4 feet, is clear blue with branching habit ; and Harry Smetham, rich porcelain blue, is semi-double, about 5 feet.

For summer display the Phloxes will be appreciated, and Le Mahdi, Ouragan, Derviche, and Lord Rayleigh are good blues of varying shades. In many ways the Anchusas

BLUE FLOWER BORDER

may be considered as being among the best of herbaceous plants, therefore those two varieties, Dropmore and Opal, should be boldly massed. For planting in clumps at the back of the border, or alternatively as a row to form a background, Sweet Peas are indispensable; Mrs. Tom Jones, bright blue, and Lord Nelson, deep blue self, are suitable varieties.

Canterbury Bells must be made use of, and various blue Irises will be planted. Lupins, too, must find a place, and Salvia azurea and Eryngium (Sea Hollies), together with Echinops Ritro (the Globe Thistle), will enhance the beauty of the border.

Among the annuals, Asters and Ten-week Stocks will be included, but few people realize how effective the Viscarias are when massed; for the blue border, Bright Blue is the best variety. Convolvulus minor is another plant deserving wider cultivation, and seeds of the variety Dark Blue, sown in open spaces in the front of the border in May, would produce effective clumps of bloom. The pretty Cornflower-blue flowers of Nigella Miss Jekyll (Love-in-a-Mist) should need no recommendation, especially as the plant is almost as desirable for its foliage as for its flowers. Blue Verbenas and Phlox Drummondi, blue Pansies, annual Larkspurs, Salvia patens, annual Cornflowers and the pretty Flaxes (Linum) all contribute to a riot of colour in the blue flower border during summer.

For autumn display one of the Monkshoods (Aconitum Wilsoni) is invaluable, and in the blue border it is useful for filling up the somewhat large gaps caused by the decline of the Delphiniums. A glance at the plan will show that the Monkshoods have been massed close to those summer-flowering plants. The best include Californicum, 5 feet, rich deep blue flowers; Sparkesi, 6 feet, indigo blue; and Wilsoni, a comparatively new sort which will attain a height of 7 feet in good soil, having splendid spikes of hood-shaped, blue flowers in September. These Monkshoods are attractive from August until the end of October.

The Monkshood (Aconitum Napellus), an excellent blue-flowered hardy perennial

BLUE FLOWER BORDER

The Michaelmas Daisies are at their best during the declining days of summer and autumn. Among the blue varieties are : Hon. Edith Gibbs, 5 feet, with lovely pale blue flowers charmingly displayed on drooping branches ; Comeliness, 4 feet, pale blue ; and Paragon, 4 feet, rich blue. Climax, 5 feet, must not be missed, for this is the finest light blue Aster yet offered to the public. Little Boy Blue, 4 feet, and Little Bo-Peep, 4 feet, are splendid silvery-grey Asters ; and Comet, 2 feet, deep blue, is one of the best dwarf varieties. Other autumn flowers in the blue border will be the second blooms of the Violas, Canterbury Bells, and Anchusa, all of which produce a number of flowers in the autumn, if the fading summer blooms have been removed systematically. Salvia patens will still be in bloom during autumn.

CHAPTER XIV

A White Flower Border

ALTHOUGH one does not often see a border devoted entirely to white flowers, such an arrangement may be made with beautiful effect. Those who have experimented with the massing of white flowers generally agree that the full beauty of many choice white plants is appreciated only when seen apart from that of other colours. The finest example of a white garden that I have seen was in a garden enclosed by four fairly high brick walls. At the foot of each wall there was a border 2 feet in width, while the rest of the enclosure was a nicely-kept lawn. In the centre of the lawn an old sun-dial stood, and at its base rough paving-stones had been laid in such a fashion that crevices were formed. These crevices provided ideal pockets for carpeting plants, such as Campanula carpatica alba. On the walls white Clematis and Climbing Roses clambered informally, whilst in the borders were the stately Madonna Lilies and occasional standards of the white Rose Frau Karl Druschki. Garden seats, painted white, stood invitingly on the well-kept grass, and on a hot sunny afternoon this quaint garden seemed to combine the good qualities of daintiness, restfulness, and beauty. The massing of white flowers, if rare, is justifiable and desirable.

There are so many white flowers that the reader who contemplates planting a white border need not adhere strictly to the plants enumerated in the plan illustrating this chapter. In making the plan the idea has been to group the various plants in such a way as to secure a display of bloom in spring, summer and autumn. Many interesting variations are

A White Flower Border—First Part

A White Flower Border—Second Part

A White Flower Border—Third Part

possible, however, and still the border may be floriferous during the three seasons mentioned.

Starting at the back of the border, the Rose lover may dispense with the Hollyhocks and substitute two Pillar Roses. Then it must be admitted that the lovely white Verbascum Miss Willmott has strong claims to recognition, and those who admire this plant could well include it at the expense of the Dahlias. It is, however, in the front of the border where the most sweeping variations are possible. Whatever is done in this direction I strongly recommend that Allwoodii Harold be retained. The flowers of this large double white "Perpetual Pink" are produced in phenomenal numbers, and the length of the stems and the soundness of the calyx combine to make this interesting plant indispensable for garden decoration generally, particularly for the foreground of the herbaceous border.

Great use should be made of the Pheasant's Eye and Gardenia flowered Narcissi, and the Darwin Tulip White Queen for spring decoration of the border. Early Single Tulips such as L'Immacule, White Pottebakker and Queen of Whites may also be made full use of, and the gaps caused by the dying off of these bulbs in late spring may be filled by white annual flowers which have been previously sown in slight warmth under glass. Among these annuals Phlox Drummondi takes a leading place, the varieties Snowball and Purity producing immense trusses of pure white flowers. The Verbena Giant White is no less beautiful, and Sweet Sultan Giant White might be made greater use of, considering the usefulness of the flowers for cutting purposes. The Scabious, although strictly speaking a perennial, is, like the popular Snapdragon, better treated as an annual. The Annual Poppy White Swan and the white variety of the Giant Perfection Ten-week Stock are indispensable for a white border. Double white Petunias are handsome; white Nemesia Suttoni is exceptionally showy; Cosmea White Queen is good in late summer, and Candytuft Improved

Flowers of the Herbaceous Phlox

White Spiral grand for a July display. There still remain many fine white Annual Asters, whilst among biennials Sweet William Giant White and white Canterbury Bells should on no account be missed.

The Michaelmas Daisies shown in the plan are all good. Avalanche is of erect habit and usually attains a height of 4 feet; Perfection is a little taller with branched growth; Desire is a variety 4 feet high and a compact grower; and Star Shower, of the same height, has pendulous growth. All the Phloxes mentioned are standard varieties. The Japanese Anemones need no recommendation, and the same remark applies to the Madonna Lilies.

The Astilbes, Spiraeas, and Lupins are included not only for their choice flowers but also on account of their charming foliage. Chrysanthemums maximum Mrs. Lowthian Bell and King Edward VII must be included; their Daisy-like flowers are useful for garden and indoor decoration. There are not many white Delphiniums, but Moerheimi is a fine variety with a long flowering period.

CHAPTER XV

A Border of Mauve Flowers

IN the height of summer a border devoted to mauve flowers is charming, and there is a greater display of bloom in the autumn than one would expect from a casual examination of the plans illustrating this chapter. The Michaelmas Daisies then make a brave display. Statice latifolia (Sea Lavender) is effective, the clumps of Sweet Peas will still have flowers if the plants have been looked after properly ; and by keeping faded blooms removed, the Canterbury Bells, Erigeron speciosus and the Violas produce a second crop of flowers.

For spring, plants of the Single Tulip Molière (lilac-mauve) should be planted in autumn on the ground rendered vacant by the clearing of summer flowering annuals, and plentiful use might also be made of May-flowering Tulips, such as Louisiana (a fine mauve), Rev. Ewbank (mauve, shaded bronze), and Ronald Gunn (grey mauve). Clumps of mauve Crocuses are, of course, very useful. The Violas shown (Eileen and Maggie Mott) are beautiful mauve varieties. The Alpine Phlox, G. F. Wilson, is a showy mauve plant, and Aubrietia H. Marshall is also worthy of inclusion. It will be seen that the border should be attractive from the end of April until the end of September, and during the summer months the display will be glorious.

The success of the mauve flower border may be assured by planting the Delphiniums recommended. Mrs. Colin McIven (5 feet) has semi-double flowers of heliotrope shade ; Mrs. Shirley (5 feet) is an effective lilac-mauve ; Sergeant Beranger (5 feet), double flowers of clear mauve ; Lilacina (4 feet), deep lilac-mauve ; Lavanda (5 feet), rosy lavender ;

and Statuaire Rude (5 feet), pale heliotrope, are grand varieties.

There are some suitable Phloxes, such varieties as Esperance (4 feet), pale mauve, white centre ; Selection (4 feet),

A Mauve and Purple Corner in the Garden planted with Clematis, Stocks, Nepeta and Salvia nemorosa

rich mauve, white centre ; Orientale (4 feet), soft rosy mauve, and Sinbad (2 feet), lilac-mauve, all being worthy of inclusion. Among the Michaelmas Daisies, Glory of Colwall (4 feet), a semi-double pale lavender, is one of the best. Beauty of Colwall (5 feet), deep lavender, is equally as good, while

A Mauve Flower Border—First Part

A Mauve Flower Border—Second Part

MAUVE FLOWER BORDER

Triumph (5 feet), deep mauve, produces its flowers on long sprays, and is very desirable. Edwin Beckett (4 feet) is a delicate mauve variety, Nancy Ballard (4 feet) is purplish mauve, and Wm. Marshall (4 feet) is a clear mauve ; all are worth growing with the taller sorts already mentioned.

Sea Lavender is desirable as the blooms may be dried for winter, and varieties of Iris Germanica, such as John Bull, Mrs. Reuthe, and Cordelia, will make an excellent early summer display if they are massed. The Erigerons named are very effective, so too are mauve Canterbury Bells and Campanula Hendersoni, while Nepeta Mussinii is suitable for the edge of the border.

Free use must be made of mauve annuals to fill the gaps among the perennials, and tall-growing plants are available in mauve Larkspurs and Scabious, the latter making splendid border plants. The mauve variety of the Giant Anemone flowered annual Aster should not be missed, for this attains a height of 2 feet and has a vigorous branching habit. Perhaps even more desirable are the Single mauve Asters, which are very beautiful. Then there are the useful Sweet Sultan, a suitable variety being Giant Mauve ; the mauve variety of Giant Perfection Ten-week Stocks, and that splendid Phlox Drummondi, Mauve Beauty. Mauve Linaria is highly attractive ; Godetia Double Mauve is easily grown and is very effective, and Candytuft Lilac Queen might also find a place. Annuals at the back of the border are well represented by the Sweet Peas R. F. Felton, King Mauve and Austin Frederick Improved.

CHAPTER XVI

A Pink and Rose Flower Border

IF a border is to be devoted to flowers of one colour it is doubtful if any better effects can be obtained than by the massing of pink and rose shades. The general appearance in the height of summer of such a border is entrancing. Many variations of the accompanying plan are possible; for example, some of the Dahlias may be excluded and clumps of such Sweet Peas as Hawlmark Pink and Doris used instead. Then, again, the Roses recommended may be trained on a background of trellis work instead of on pillars.

Some people complain that a border of one colour is attractive only for a limited period. This contention however, may easily be refuted. By making use of the plants indicated on the plan one may rely on a fine display from early summer until well into the autumn. Perhaps the spring display will not be very striking, yet charming effects may be secured by Wallflowers Rosy Gem and Pink Dwarf Bedder. The Godetias recommended may be followed by the little-known pink Forget-me-nots. Anemone Rose de Nice may also be used, and Tulips, such as Queen of the Pinks, Proserpine, and Le Matelas (among the singles), and Queen of the Roses, Lady Palmerston and Salvator Rosa (of the doubles). Autumn plantations of Pink Hyacinths may also be made, so that the spring display need not be niggardly.

In early summer quite a number of fine flowering plants will display their charms in the pink and rose border. Pride of place must be given to Sweet William Pink Beauty. This salmon-pink variety should find a place in every perennial

The Grecian Mallow (Sidalcea), a handsome hardy border flower

Pink and Rose Flower Border—First Part

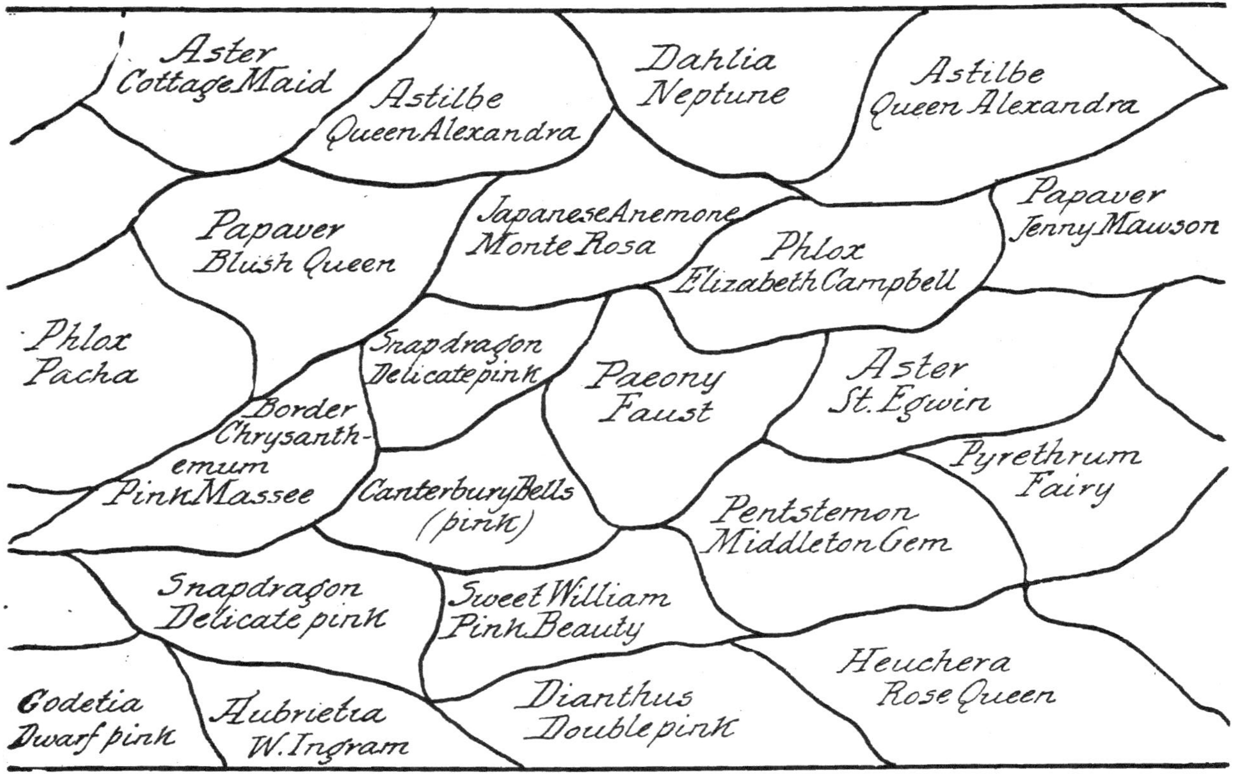

Pink and Rose Flower Border—Second Part

Pink and Rose Flower Border—Third Part

PINK AND ROSE FLOWER BORDER

border, for it makes a delightful display. The Canterbury Bells will also be in bloom during early summer, and a later display may be secured by cutting off the dead blooms. Then what of the gorgeous Paeonies ? Sorts such as Jules Lebon, Indispensable and Faust should be made use of. Other worthy plants in this early summer pageant are the Pyrethrums and Heucheras, shown on the plan, and Allwoodii " Robert " is also attractive.

Provided the site has been deeply dug and liberally manured, the presence of Phloxes ensures a brilliant July and August display. Varieties such as Sheriff Ivory, Selma, Fort de France, and Elizabeth Campbell are attractive if given rich soil. Lupinus roseus and Spiraea venusta are good border plants, and far greater use should be made of the last-named, for, in addition to its producing waving plumes of beautiful flowers, the foliage is distinctly decorative. The Astilbe is a closely allied plant and equally desirable, the variety Queen Alexandra being very charming. Lavatera Olbia is a tall and handsome Tree Mallow. The Oriental Poppies Blush Queen and Jenny Mawson are also beautiful, whilst Hollyhock Lady Bailey has charming colouring. Many perennial Asters are included to ensure an autumn display.

CHAPTER XVII

A Border of Yellow Flowers

FEW people make sufficient use of yellow flowers, a fact that is surprising when one reflects that for at least nine months in the year it is possible to enliven the garden with flowers of this colour. There is the yellow Crocus in February and March, whilst the perennial Sunflowers are often very attractive until well into November. To those who have never tried a grouping of yellow-flowered plants the result obtained will be a revelation of beauty.

On the accompanying plan it will be seen that several annuals are arranged towards the front. Their association with perennials may be advocated strongly when yellow borders are being planted, because when they are cleared away in autumn the spaces rendered vacant may be filled with yellow Wallflowers such as Cloth of Gold. It is also possible to make use of Daffodils and Crocuses, so that the yellow border may be attractive in spring. In addition to the Wallflowers and Daffodils are the Doronicums with their golden-yellow Daisy-like flowers, the Alyssum, and that dwarf plant Adonis vernalis. The last-named is more often accommodated on rockeries, but it makes a charming display when grouped on the edge of a flower border. It rarely exceeds a foot in height and it is early flowering, the golden-yellow flowers appearing in March.

If the accompanying plan is followed the golden-yellow flowers of spring will be succeeded in early summer by the various Violas and Aquilegia chrysantha. This is a fine border plant, the long-spurred golden-yellow flowers being displayed above elegant foliage. Anthemis tinctoria Kelwayi

YELLOW FLOWER BORDER

is attractive, and everyone knows how useful the Coreopsis is for garden display and indoor decoration. Gaillardias have so many friends that little need be said to justify their inclusion in a border of yellow flowers, but it should be re-

One of the Coneflowers (Rudbeckia Newmanii),
a useful yellow border flower

membered that the pure yellow variety, Lady Rolleston, is most suitable.

I cannot imagine a more stately and beautiful plant for the back of the border than Verbascum olympicum, but

Yellow Flower Border—First Part

Yellow Flower Border—Second Part

Yellow Flower Border—Third Part

YELLOW FLOWER BORDER

those who do not like this flower may replace it with that splendid double Hollyhock Queen of the Yellows.

Rose Shower of Gold is very effective in the background if grown on pillars or trellis work. The Trollius merits a place in a yellow border if only on account of the handsome foliage, but the flowers are very beautiful also. The tall bearded Irises must be included, and Iris aurea suits us best,

A Handsome Torch Lily (Kniphofia caulescens)

because it is a fine golden-yellow sort and quite distinct Snapdragons Yellow Prince and Cloth of Gold make a good summer display.

Mignonette is incomparable for fragrance, and the flowers, too, are beautiful. Grow the varieties Giant Yellow and Cloth of Gold. Another annual shown is Nasturtium Cloth of Gold, and this is really effective. The Kniphofias, or Red Hot Pokers, must be included. Meteor and Star of

Baden are both suitable varieties. Heleniums are fine border plants, easy to grow and very compact in habit. Riverton Beauty and Riverton Gem are both good varieties. The Lupins must be grown to be fully appreciated, and Somerset, the variety shown, makes a bold display of yellow.

To provide yellow blooms in autumn there are many good plants, but possibly the Rudbeckias or Coneflowers take precedence over them all. At the back of the border they will prove strikingly effective, especially if the varieties Golden Glow and Autumn Glory are grown. Despite the fact that the flowers soon fade, the Golden Rods are indispensable; Golden Wings, the variety shown on the plan, is very effective and about the last to flower.

A garden without Dahlias would not be very bright during September, therefore yellow varieties are freely shown. There are some people, however, who are not fond of the Dahlia, and they might substitute clumps of Sweet Peas, in the varieties Majestic Cream and Matchless. Border Chrysanthemums are indispensable, and for a yellow border few varieties can excel Carrie, Horace Martin and Tapis d'Or. Finally there are Perennial Sunflowers (Helianthus), and these are glorious for late autumn effects. In favourable seasons these plants bear their beautiful golden-yellow flowers from September until November is well advanced.

CHAPTER XVIII

A Border of Red Flowers

To obtain a brilliant display one cannot do better than plant a border with flowers of crimson, scarlet and orange. Flowers of all these shades are included in the accompanying plan, but for the sake of brevity and convenience the whole has been described as " A Border of Red Flowers." A glance at the plan will show that some of the best herbaceous plants have been included, but of course variations are possible.

If a spring display is desired, the spaces occupied by annuals during summer may be filled in autumn with Wallflowers such as Fire King, Giant Vulcan and Blood Red. Tulips of merit for this border are Fred Moore, orange, shaded scarlet; Joost Van Vondel, cherry-red; Koh-i-noor, velvety crimson; Sparklet, scarlet; and Bacchus, crimson, all singles. Gala, crimson-scarlet; Macrospeila, rose-crimson; Panorama, orange-red; and Orange Globe are Darwin (May-flowering) Tulips, suitable for inclusion.

In early summer the Aubrietias Vanguard and Fire King will be attractive. Heuchera sanguinea bears its graceful spikes of bright red flowers in May, and the Double Daisy " Rubens " will also attract attention at that season. The Paeonies mentioned are all good, and Pyrethrums like James Kelway, Ernest Kelway, and Lord Rosebery have only to be grown to be appreciated. Geum Mrs. Bradshaw is a splendid border plant producing scarlet flowers from May to September. The Sweet William Scarlet Beauty is no less beautiful, and it gains many new friends annually. As an edging plant Mimulus cardinalis (the Monkey Flower)

Red Flower Border—First Part

Red Flower Border—Second Part

Red Flower Border—Third Part

should be more popular, producing as it does large crimson flowers from May to the end of August. During July and August the border will be gay, for the Sweet Peas Charity, Royal Scot, Gloriosa and Grenadier will be at their best, and rivalling them will be those fine pillar Roses, Excelsa and Hiawatha. The first-named Rose has dense and glossy foliage, while the carmine-scarlet flowers are freely produced. Hiawatha is a beautiful Rose with single crimson flowers.

By massing Kniphofia (Red Hot Poker) as shown in the plan, a striking effect will be obtained, for the flowers of this plant are particularly handsome. Kniphofia caulescens is distinct from the others, owing to its ornamental, Yucca-like foliage; the cream coloured flowers with glowing red tops are freely produced from late June until mid-September. Pfitzeri is a rather dwarf Tritoma with coral-red flowers appearing in the months of September and October. K. nobilis is another autumn beauty with spikes of brilliant scarlet; whilst rufa, coral-red, blooms from June to August. It will be seen that the Red Hot Pokers are indispensable for a red border, because they enliven both summer and autumn and have bold and attractive foliage.

Perennial Phloxes add greatly to the summer glory of this border, and varieties like Tragédie, red; Lord Kelvin, red; Coquelicot, scarlet; and Robert le Diable, red, are very showy. Dictamnus Fraxinella (Burning Bush) is a striking perennial, and must be included. The same applies to Monarda didyma (Bergamot), with scarlet flowers in summer. Lychnis chalcedonica is an old favourite, and its dense heads of scarlet flowers are so beautiful in July and August that we must include it. Oriental Poppies with their graceful foliage and truly gorgeous flowers cannot be omitted, and varieties like Royal Scarlet and Beauty of Livermere are fine when massed. The first-named Poppy attains a height of 4 feet, and has orange-scarlet flowers, while Beauty of Livermere is notable for its large red

Border Chrysanthemum Fée Parisienne
(Rose Pink)

Border Chrysanthemum Cream Perriere
(Cream Yellow)

blooms, on stems about 4 feet high. Chelone barbata is a useful perennial with tubular scarlet flowers from June to August, while everyone likes the scarlet flowers of Lobelia cardinalis.

Annuals such as Phlox Drummondi, Nicotiana affinis (Tobacco Plant), Godetia Double Crimson, Mignonette Giant Red, Aster Southcote Beauty, Larkspur Rosy Scarlet, and Snapdragons Orange King, Crimson King, and Tall Crimson should find a place in this border.

The Red Hot Pokers will be attractive during the autumn months, and they will be supplemented by Montbretias. There are not many good red Michaelmas Daisies, but the inclusion of Mrs. J. F. Rayner with its rose-crimson flowers will ensure a fine display. Dahlias such as F. W. Fellowes, orange-scarlet, and H. H. Thomas, crimson, will be at their zenith in September. The pillar Roses will produce a few flowers, and the beautiful double Hollyhocks Victor, crimson-scarlet; William Archer, crimson; Fire King, bright red; and Crimson Queen continue attractive until frost puts an end to them. Reserve plants of Border Chrysanthemums such as Goacher's Crimson could take the place of some of the fading annuals in August, and if this were done the show of red flowers in autumn would be improved.

CHAPTER XIX

A Border of Annual Flowers

A BORDER filled with annuals provides a brilliant display, while many of the flowers are invaluable for cutting. Annuals are grouped in two divisions, hardy and half-hardy, the former being sown in March, April or May, where they are to flower, and the latter in warmth under glass during February, March and April.

Sweet Peas are, of course, hardy, and may be sown in the open ground in March, but better results are obtained by sowing in pots or boxes during the first week in February; the seedlings must be given plenty of fresh air to keep them sturdy. Many beautiful annual Asters are shown, and these are indispensable for cutting purposes and garden display. To raise sturdy plants the seeds should be sown in cold frames or shallow boxes about the middle of March, cool conditions suiting the plants best. Ten-week Stocks may be sown at the same time. The soil for Ten-week Stocks should be light and not too rich, otherwise the seedlings may "damp off." Verbenas, Snapdragons, Phlox Drummondi, Nicotiana affinis, Scabious, Salpiglossis and Annual Chrysanthemums should be sown in slight warmth in February, choosing shallow boxes as seed receptacles, and transplanting the seedlings to other boxes as growth advances. Larkspurs, Clarkias, and Sweet Sultans are better if sown thinly in a cold frame in March and the seedlings transplanted to the border about the third week in May.

That beautiful annual Nigella Miss Jekyll (Love-in-a-Mist) is not easily transplanted and succeeds better if sown

A Blue Sweet Pea—Mrs. T. Jones

in the border during March. Godetias may be freely sown in the open at the same time, as also may that quick-flowering annual Leptosyne Stillmani. The first week in April is a suitable time for an out of door sowing of Viscaria. Nemophila, Mignonette, Malope, Annual Poppies, Helichrysum (Everlasting Flowers), Candytuft and Cornflower. If the Balsams and Calendulas (Pot Marigolds) are cultivated it is better to sow them in the greenhouse during April and transplant to the border in May. If the colour grouping

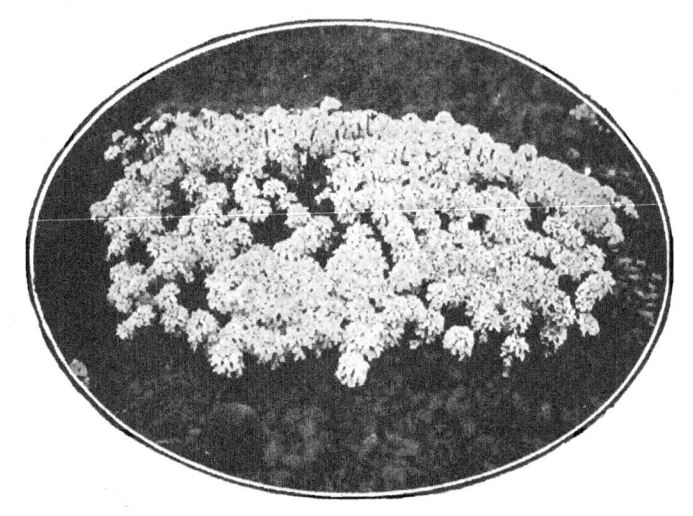

Candytuft, an indispensable hardy annual

shown in the plan is followed, the effect will be beautiful. Never attempt the outdoor sowing of annuals when the soil is sodden. Wait until it is dry. If the soil is heavy, lighten it by adding old and dry potting soil. Rake the surface down to a fine tilth, sow thinly and cover the seeds lightly. Thin the seedlings early—annuals are usually spoilt through overcrowding. When sowing half-hardy annuals under glass use a light sandy compost and keep the seedlings fairly close to the glass, otherwise they will become "drawn" and weak.

Border of Annual Flowers—First Part

Border of Annual Flowers—Second Part

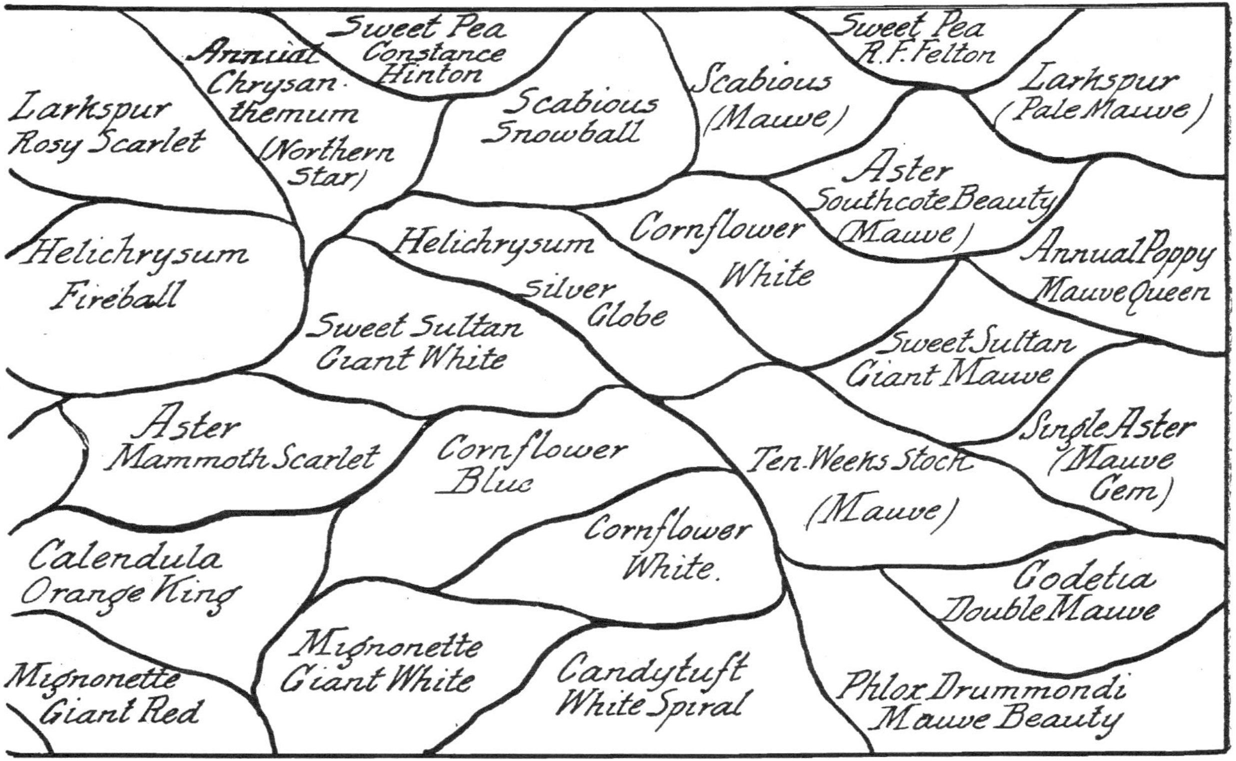

Border of Annual Flowers—Third Part

CHAPTER XX

Shrubs for the Flower Border

THE presence of a few shrubs in the flower border adds to its interest, gives stability of form and outline and additional attractiveness during the summer months, while saving it from the reproach of being wholly without charm in winter and early spring. Some shrubs bloom in winter, others in spring, summer and autumn, and if a careful selection is made it will be found well worth while to include some of them in the scheme when planting a hardy flower border. They must be so arranged that they are seen above the herbaceous perennials, even when these are in full bloom, otherwise much of their peculiar value is lost. They are particularly useful for preventing a monotonous outline, such as is apt to result when herbaceous perennials alone are used; by planting them so that they outcrop, as it were, among plants of somewhat lower growth, the desired effect is obtained, and the display gains in variety and interest.

There are many flowering shrubs suitable for the purpose in view. Of those that bloom in winter one must choose the Witch Hazel named Hamamelis mollis, which bears numerous curiously twisted yellow flowers in the depth of winter, and of which the leaves do not detract from the flower display in summer.

Of shrubs that blossom in spring the first choice should be one of the Golden Bells—Forsythia intermedia or spectabilis, preferably the latter, which bears its golden, bell-shaped flowers very freely and provides a brilliant display in April. If room can be found for a few bulbs of Grape Hyacinth

SHRUBS FOR THE FLOWER BORDER 101

(Muscari Heavenly Blue), these being planted in autumn, there will be a delightful flower show of gold over a carpet of blue in spring.

Of summer flowering shrubs few are more beautiful than the double-flowered Mock Oranges, such as Philadelphus Rosace, Virginale and Boule d'Argent; their slender branches become wreathed in lovely bloom, and if planted near blue

The Rhododendron is the Finest Hardy Flowering Shrub, and may well be planted in the Mixed Border

flowered plants, such as the Delphiniums, which bloom at the same time, the result is fascinating. Philadelphus Lemoinei erectus, shown in the illustration, bears single flowers. Here and there a Rhododendron may be planted; its large, evergreen leaves are always attractive, while in the month of May its bunches of blossom provide an enchanting display. Of the numerous varieties in cultivation few are

H

A Free-flowering Mock Orange (Philadelphus Lemoinei Erectus)

SHRUBS FOR THE FLOWER BORDER

lovelier than Pink Pearl. If the faded flower heads are removed to prevent the formation of seed, and the soil immediately above the roots is mulched with leaf-mould each spring, this shrub may be relied upon to bloom well almost every year.

A standard Rose or two of one of the free-growing varieties, such as W. A. Richardson or Madame Alfred Carrière (white), look well if they are on tall stems and are planted towards the back of the border. They need to be securely staked, for they make large "heads," and when in full leaf are liable to be blown down and damaged by high wind.

The Crimson Spiraea Anthony Waterer, which grows some 2 feet high and blooms freely in July and August, is a splendid little shrub, and a small group might well be made of it; the shoots should be pruned almost to the base in spring, as it is the fresh growths that produce the flowers. The hardy Fuchsias, macrostemma, Riccartonii, and gracilis, make large bushes and bear reddish blooms in late summer; they too are worth including, but they must be so placed that they do not clash with those of neighbouring plants; they are best among light coloured flowers.

Spiraea Thunbergii is a shrub 4 to 5 feet high, having small white flowers in spring, and graceful, light green foliage; it sets off richly coloured flowers to great advantage. For the sake of its pink buds and white blossom in autumn and winter, room might well be found for a bush or two of Laurustinus.

CHAPTER XXI

The Chief Hardy Border Flowers

Acanthus.—Distinguished by large ornamental, deeply cut leaves, and producing flower stems 2 to 4 feet high; the flowers are of purple and white colouring. The best kinds are longifolius, 3 to 4 feet, mollis, 3 feet, and spinosus, 2 to 3 feet. These plants become established slowly; they are not likely to flower in less than two or three years.

Achillea.—The chief border kind is Achillea Ptarmica, of which the varieties The Pearl and Perry's White are commonly grown. These have small, double white flowers, and grow about 2 feet high. A. Millefolium roseum is rose coloured, and A. Eupatorium has yellow heads of flower.

Aconitum (Monkshood).—Tall perennials, most of which have blue flowers and bloom in late summer and autumn. Aconitum Napellus (July—September, 4 to 5 feet), Fischeri (September, 3 feet), and Wilsoni (September, 5 to 6 feet) are some of the finest sorts. The white variety (album) and the blue and white variety (bicolor) of the common Monkshood bloom in July; the last named is particularly attractive.

Alstroemeria (Peruvian or Herb Lily).—A group of tuberous-rooted plants which need light, well-drained soil and a warm, sunny position. They dislike being disturbed, and benefit by a covering of leaf-mould in autumn. They flower in July-August. The chief sorts are aurantiaca, orange, marked with red and carmine; pelegrina, variously coloured; and chilensis hybrida, crimson, orange, yellow, and other shades. They reach a height of 2 to 3 feet.

Althaea (Hollyhock).—Indispensable flowers for the

CHIEF HARDY FLOWERS

mixed border. Their tall stems towering above most other plants add greatly to the charm of the display. There are many named varieties, with double or single flowers. The best way to grow them is from seed; this may be sown in a cold frame in June to provide flowering plants for the following year, the plants being wintered in a frame; or seed can be sown in a heated glasshouse in January to

White Milfoil (Achillea The Pearl)

provide flowering plants the same year. Hollyhocks need deeply dug and rich soil if they are to do really well.

Alyssum (Madwort).—The best two perennials for the border are Alyssum saxatile, bright yellow, and the variety citrinum, which has lemon-yellow flowers. They do best in well-drained soil, and are brilliant spring flowering plants for the front of the border.

Anchusa (Alkanet).—These are brilliant blue-flowered

perennials. Those chiefly grown are varieties of **Anchusa italica**, named Dropmore and Opal, the former being rich blue and the latter light blue. Although they are perennial in some soils, in others they are of little use after having blossomed. They are, however, easily propagated by digging up the fleshy roots, cutting these into pieces 4 inches or so long, and planting them in a box of soil in a frame.

Anemone (Windflower).—Of the many kinds of Anemone in cultivation the Japanese Anemone (Anemone Japonica) and its varieties are most useful for border planting. These plants should remain undisturbed for many years. They do well in partial shade. Some of the best sorts are japonica, white, 2 to 3 feet; Queen Charlotte, rose, semi-double; Prince Heinrich, rose crimson, semi-double; and Lord Ardilaun, white, semi-double. They flower in August and September.

Anthemis (Chamomile).—Easily grown summer blooming plants bearing numerous yellow Daisy-like flowers and reaching a height of about 2 feet. Anthemis tinctoria and its varieties Kelwayi and E. C. Buxton are chiefly worth growing.

Arabis.—The double white Arabis is a valuable spring flowering plant for use near the margin of the border. It is improved by being well cut back as soon as the flowers are over.

Armeria (Thrift).—This is one of the best of all edging plants. It forms a compact evergreen tuft, and in June is smothered with rose-red flowers. The variety laucheana has flowers of brighter colour than the common kind. It is best increased by division in September.

Artemisia (Wormwood).—The finest of the Artemisias grown for their flowers is A. lactiflora; this reaches a height of 5 feet, and in September bears a profusion of creamy white flowers. It is a most decorative plant. Artemisia Abrotanum is the Old Man, an old-fashioned plant with grey, fragrant leaves.

The Japanese Anemone

HARDY BORDER FLOWERS

Aster (Michaelmas Daisy).—The Starworts or Michaelmas Daisies are invaluable for providing a display in the mixed border during late summer and autumn. They vary in height from 18 inches to 5 or 6 feet or more; some have large, handsome blooms, while others are smothered in tiny flowers. The colour range is now a wide one, from white through lavender and rose-pink to purple. Most varieties

Astilbe, or Goat's Beard, is a handsome border flower

have single flowers, but there are now several sorts with double flowers. The following are a few of the best: acris, lavender blue, 2 feet; Amellus King George, violet blue, 2 feet; Lil Fardell, rose-pink, 5 feet; Perry's Favourite, lilac-pink, $2\frac{1}{2}$ feet; William Marshall, 4 feet; Delight, very small white flowers, 3 feet; Beauty of Colwall, double, lavender-blue, $4\frac{1}{3}$ feet; Wonder of Colwall, pale lavender-blue, 5 feet; Keston Blue, blue, 5 feet; Mrs. J. F. Rayner,

CHIEF HARDY FLOWERS

rose crimson, 5 feet; and Climax, light blue, 5 to 6 feet. They come into bloom in approximately this order. Michaelmas Daisies, if left undisturbed for several seasons, develop into splendid clumps and then yield a profusion of flowers. They should be taken up and divided every four years or so.

Astilbe (Goat's Beard).—The Astilbes are Spiraea-like plants which bear tall, plume-like inflorescences of white or coloured blossoms in summer and are most decorative. As they are rather untidy after the flowers are over they should be so placed that later flowering plants will hide them to some extent. A few of the best are vesta, rose-pink, 4 to 5 feet, June; grandis, white, 4 to 6 feet, August to September; and rivularis, white, 4 feet, June, July. They must be watered very freely in summer, and a partially shaded position is an advantage.

Aubrietia.—This beautiful spring flowering, low growing plant is often used with good effect at the margin of the border, especially if the edging is of stone. It thrives much better in rather light soil than in heavy ground, so plenty of grit should be mixed with the soil at planting time. Some of the best varieties are Dr. Mules, purple; Mrs. Lloyd Edwards, crimson; Pritchard's A1, purple; Fire King, crimson; Bridesmaid, blush; and Moerheimi, rose.

Bocconia (Plume Poppy).—Bocconia cordata is a tall, handsome flowering plant that cannot be omitted from the large border, but it is too vigorous for a small border. It has decorative, grey green leaves, and produces plumes of cream coloured flowers which reach a height of 6 to 8 feet or more.

Campanula (Bellflower).—There are so many splendid border Campanulas that every garden must have some of them if it is to look its best in June and July. They are easily grown in deep, moderately rich soil, and prefer a partially shaded position; at any rate they must not be planted where they are liable to suffer from drought. A few invaluable kinds are persicifolia, blue, 3 feet; persicifolia alba, white, 3 feet ; Moerheimi, blue, 3 feet ; Telham Beauty, blue, 4 to 5 feet ; grandis, blue, 2 to 3 feet ; lactiflora, blue, 4 feet ; lactiflora alba, white, 4 feet ; and latifolia macrantha, violet blue, 4 to 5 feet. Then there are the Canterbury

The Carpathian Bellflower (Campanula carpatica)

Bells in white, rose and purple blue ; these are biennials, and are raised from seed sown in May and June to flower the following year.

Carnation (*see* Dianthus).

Catananche (Cupidone).—A decorative and graceful

The Finest Variety of Peach-leaved Bellflower (Campanula Telham Beauty)

border perennial, growing about 2 feet high, and bearing in summer an abundance of blue flowers on long wiry stems. Catananche caerulea is the kind commonly grown.

Centaurea (Knapweed).—The annual Centaureas or Cornflowers are better known than the perennial kinds, but the latter comprise several good border plants, such as dealbata, rose purple, 2 feet ; glastifolia, yellow, 4 feet ; montana, flowers of various shades, 2 feet, and ruthenica, pale yellow, 4 feet.

Centranthus (Valerian).—This is a most useful plant, for it has brightly coloured flowers in abundance and remains attractive from June to September. Centranthus ruber is the common Valerian, having rose-red flowers, but those of the variety coccineus are a brighter and better colour, and this should be grown.

Chrysanthemum.—From the gardening point of view there are two distinct sets of Chrysanthemum—those with Chrysanthemum-like flowers which are so valuable in late summer and autumn, and others having large white, Marguerite-like blooms during the summer months, and popularly known as Shasta Daisies. The latter cannot well be left out of any planting scheme, for they bloom very freely, making an attractive display for some weeks, and they are easily grown. The typical kind is Chrysanthemum maximum, but improved varieties are King Edward, Mrs. C. Lowthian Bell, Triumph, and William Robinson ; all have large white flowers, and reach a height of 3 feet or so. The Border Chrysanthemums are invaluable for bringing colour to the border when so many other flowers have faded. If room cannot be found for them in the border proper until some of the earlier plants, such as Sweet William and Canterbury Bell are over, they must be grown on a reserve border ; they can be lifted without damage if well watered the day before and taken up carefully. A selection of varieties is as follows : Madame Masse, lilac mauve ; Horace Martin, yellow ; Fée Parisienne, rosy mauve ; Harrie, bronze orange ;

CHIEF HARDY FLOWERS

Elstob Yellow, yellow; Carrie, yellow; Diana, bronze orange; Glory of Merstham, pink; Lichfield Purple, purple; Minnie Carpenter, terra cotta; Robbie Burns, salmon pink; Lichfield Pink, pink; and Wells' Crimson. They should be left undisturbed for two or three years and then develop into fine clumps. It is wise to cover the clumps with old ashes in autumn. Propagation is easily effected by cuttings in February and March.

A Dainty Bellflower for the Border Edge—Campanula pusilla

Cimicifuga (Fleabane).—These plants have decorative leaves and produce racemes of white flowers on stems 3 to 4 feet high. The best are simplex, July; racemosa, August, and japonica, July.

Coreopsis (Tickseed).—The finest Coreopsis for the border is C. grandiflora, but, unfortunately, it is not a true perennial in all gardens, particularly where the soil is heavy. It grows about 3 feet high, and produces a profusion of golden-yellow, Marguerite-like flowers in July; if the faded blooms are picked off regularly the plant remains attractive for weeks. Coreopsis grandiflora is easily raised from seed sown in a box of soil in a frame, or out of doors in May or June, to provide flowering plants for the following summer. Coreopsis verticillata and C. lanceolata are two other useful kinds, both having yellow flowers.

Delphinium (Larkspur).—This is perhaps the finest of all hardy herbaceous plants, and certainly the best· hardy blue flowered border perennial. Its height varies, according to the varieties grown, from 3 to 4 feet to 6 to 7 feet, and in modern sorts the flowers show a wide range of colour. Most of them are of some shade of blue, but there are Delphiniums in white, mauve, and other shades. If the chief flower stems are cut off as soon as the blossoms have faded, the secondary stems or shoots will prolong the display considerably; if all flower stems are cut down to prevent the formation of seeds a number of fresh ones will develop, and will produce blooms in autumn. Delphiniums are seen at their best only when planted in ground that has been dug 2 feet deep and manured. During winter it is advisable to cover the clumps with old ashes, and if these are renewed in spring, slugs and other soil pests will do less damage than if no protection were given to the young shoots. So many varieties are to be found described in catalogues, and so many improved ones appear each year, that the reader may select those which please his fancy and suit his purse best.

Dianthus (Pink and Carnation).—The best Pinks for the mixed flower border are those comparatively new kinds called Allwoodii. They are really half Pink and half Perpetual Flowering Carnation, having been obtained by cross-breeding between those two. They grow about 18 inches high, and produce an abundance of flowers from May until late autumn. Some of the blooms are single, others are double or semi-double, and all are fragrant. Some of the chief are Harold, double white; Susan, pale lilac, dark centre; Jean, white, violet centre; Mary, pale rose pink, maroon centre; Rufus, rose red; Robert, old rose, maroon centre; and Betty, white, with reddish maroon centre. Border Carnations

A Bed of Border Carnations

are sometimes planted in the mixed border, though it is really better to grow them in a bed or series of beds by themselves. However, a few groups towards the front of the border always give pleasure, but care is necessary to see that they are not spoilt by other plants encroaching on them. They ought to be left undisturbed for two or three years, when they develop into large plants and bloom abundantly. The Perpetual Flowering Border Carnations are more suitable for the mixed flower border, since they blossom throughout a longer period. Then there are the true Perpetual Flowering Carnations, really greenhouse plants, but often used out of doors in summer. A few good varieties of Border Carnations are Border Yellow; Surrey Clove, crimson; Veldtfire, light scarlet; Lord Kitchener, white with scarlet marking; Ophelia, white with maroon marking; White Fox, white; Kelso, heliotrope and yellow; Cardinal, bright red; Grey Douglas, grey; and Daisy Walker, white flecked with red.

Sussex Pink is one of the best of the Perpetual Border Carnations, while of the true Perpetual Flowering Carnations such may be chosen as E. Allwood, scarlet; Laddie, salmon; White Enchantress; Tarzan, crimson.

Dicentra (Bleeding Heart).—This is an old plant in English gardens, and its pink and white flowers and decorative leaves make it very welcome in May. As its beauty fades early in summer, it should not have too conspicuous a position. The botanical name is Dicentra (or Dielytra) spectabilis. It grows about 2 feet high.

Dictamnus (Burning Bush).—The common Burning Bush (Dictamnus Fraxinella) grows 2 to 3 feet high, and bears reddish purple flowers in June and July; the leaves too are attractive. Dictamnus albus, the white form, is also well worth planting.

Doronicum (Leopard's Bane).—This is an invaluable yellow flowered perennial that blooms in spring and early summer. Its flowers open too early to allow of Doronicum being included in any scheme of planting for colour effect,

CHIEF HARDY FLOWERS

but its yellow, Daisy-like flowers are very bright and useful for cutting. The best kind is Doronicum excelsum (Harpur Crewe), which grows from 2 to 3 feet high and blooms in April and May. It thrives well in the shady border.

Larkspur, or Annual Delphinium

Echinacea purpurea (Purple Coneflower) is worth growing because of the reddish purple colour of its flowers, which are much like those of Rudbeckia in form. It reaches a height of 3 feet, and blooms in September.

Echinops (Globe Thistle).—The rounded, somewhat

thistle-like flower heads of Echinops render this plant conspicuous in a border; the flower heads are blue and the leaves are grey green, so the Globe Thistles are useful for supplying those neutral tints which are often of advantage in a border planted for colour effect. The best kinds are Ritro blue, 3 to 4 feet, and sphaerocephalus, steel blue flowers and silvery leaves.

Erigeron (Summer Starwort).—The Erigerons are splendid border plants, producing a wealth of Michaelmas Daisy-like blossoms during the summer months. They should certainly be well represented in a mixed border. The variety Quakeress, lavender blue, is particularly charming and flowers for many weeks. Speciosus superbus, mauve; Asa Gray, apricot buff; and Edina, white, are other good varieties. They grow from 2 to 3 feet high.

Eryngium (Sea Holly).—The Sea Hollies are among the most picturesque and distinct of border plants; their decorative leaves and metallic blue flower heads render them of great value. They thrive best in well-drained soil, though heavy ground can be made suitable by adding grit. The chief kinds, all of which are summer flowering, are alpinum, metallic blue, 3 feet; amethystinum, amethyst blue, 4 feet; Oliverianum, blue, 3 to 4 feet; and planum, small blue flower heads, 3 feet.

Funkia (Plantain Lily).—This is grown partly for its large handsome leaves, but the flowers of some kinds are attractive also. It needs deep, fairly rich soil and a partially shaded position. The leaves in various shades of green are useful for planting among gaily coloured flowers, which they set off to the best advantage. They must be kept moist at the root in summer. Subcordata grandiflora, white flowers; Sieboldiana, cream-lilac flowers; and Fortunei, with white or mauve flowers, are three good Funkias which bloom in summer. They reach a height of 20 to 24 inches. Funkia tardiflora has lilac-coloured flowers in autumn, and is less vigorous than the others named.

Eryngium, or Sea Holly

120   HARDY BORDER FLOWERS

Gaillardia.—The brilliantly coloured flowers of the Gaillardia are familiar to all garden lovers, and few plants provide richer colouring. Unfortunately, the plants are not reliable perennials, except in light or well-drained soil, and often need to be propagated annually by cuttings taken in August, or they may be raised from seeds sown in a cold frame in spring. There are many named varieties, but the flowers of all are of shades of red and yellow.

Plantain Lily (Funkia)

Galega (Goat's Rue).—Vigorous perennials which bear a profusion of small, pea-shaped flowers in summer. They reach a height of 4 feet or more. Probably the best kind is Hartlandii, which has lilac-coloured blossoms.

Geum (Avens).—One of the finest scarlet-flowered perennials is Geum Mrs. Bradshaw. This plant grows 18 to 24 inches high and bears its brilliant, semi-double Strawberry-like blooms of bright scarlet colour throughout the

A Splendid Yellow Border Flower—Helenium pumilum grandiflorum

A Showy, Free-blooming Sunflower (Helianthus Miss Mellish)

summer months, providing the faded flowers are not allowed to form seeds. It is a great improvement upon the typical kind, Geum coccineum, which has smaller flowers of similar colour, but does not bloom during such a long period. There are several yellow-flowered Geums, such for example as Orange Queen and montanum grandiflorum, which may be planted, but probably the best of all the yellow varieties is Lady Stratheden.

Gypsophila (Gauze Flower). — A well-developed plant of Gypsophila paniculata, when laden with its panicles of feathery looking blossom, is a very beautiful sight. The tiny flowers are white, but the effect of the whole mass is grey. While in itself very charming, the Gypsophila is most useful for interplanting among others of brilliant colours. The double variety is even more striking than the single kind, the flowers being larger and giving a more distinct effect. The Gypsophila thrives in any well-prepared ground, but it must not be disturbed, for it takes a year or two to become established, and annually increases in charm if left alone.

Helenium (Sneezewort).—Some of the finest flowers of late summer and autumn are found among the Heleniums. The plants grow from 2 to 5 or 6 feet high, and yield an abundance of large Daisy-like blossom in yellow and other colours. The finest of the dwarf sorts is Helenium pumilum magnificum, which grows 2 feet high and in July becomes smothered in bright yellow blooms. Among the tall growing kinds, flowering in August and September, the two best are Riverton Gem, reddish terra-cotta, and Riverton Beauty, lemon coloured. These plants develop into excellent clumps in the course of a year or two, and yield a profusion of flowers. About every four years it is as well to divide and replant.

Helianthemum (Sun Rose).—Dainty trailing evergreen plants, of which a few may be found useful for placing near the margin of the border. During June chiefly they flower profusely, and though the individual blooms are short-lived they are so numerous that an excellent and continued display is produced through the month of June. There

Cimicifuga racemosa, a valuable August-flowering plant (*see page* 113)

are many named varieties of the common Sun Rose (Helianthemum vulgare) in white, red, yellow, orange and other colours. These plants need well-drained soil, and are improved by being cut back after the flowers are over.

Helianthus (Sunflower).—The perennial Sunflowers are indispensable to the embellishment of a large flower border during late summer, for it is then that their blooms are so conspicuous. All have yellow flowers. They should, however, not be planted too freely for they spread rather rapidly, and if care is not taken they encroach on other plants and impoverish the soil. A few of the best are Miss Mellish, 6 feet; Daniel Dewar, 5 feet; orgyalis, 6 feet; Bouquet d'Or, double, 5 feet; and decapetalus, 5 feet.

Hemerocallis (Day Lily).—The Day Lilies form an evergreen tuft of narrow leaves, and the Lily-like flowers, of some shade of yellow or orange, are produced freely in June and July, when the plants are established. A few of the best kinds are aurantiaca, orange; Dumortieri, yellow and bronze; flava, bright yellow; and fulva, bronze. They reach a height of 2 to 3 feet.

Heuchera (Alum Root).—The Heucheras are dainty and invaluable plants which form low tufts of pretty leaves and blossom in May and June chiefly, the flower spikes reaching a height of from 15 to 24 inches or more. They are attractive even when out of bloom, and are indispensable for planting near the border margin. Some excellent sorts are sanguinea, scarlet; Rosamunde, pink; Flambeau, rose-scarlet; Edge Hall, rose; and sanguinea splendens, coral red.

Iberis (Evergreen Candytuft).—The perennial evergreen Candytuft (Iberis sempervirens) is an attractive, low-growing plant that bears its white flowers very freely in April and May, and may well be grouped here and there at the margin of the border. Even when out of bloom its rich green leaves are of pleasing appearance. The plants ought to be cut back after the flowering season is past. Some of the finest kinds are sempervirens, garrexiana and gibraltarica.

Iris.—The Flag Iris in its many varieties is one of the most delightful of hardy border plants, and there should be a few groups of them in every border. Not only are the flowers of modern sorts very beautiful, but the plants are decorative even when not in bloom. Their greyish leaves render them suitable for planting among highly coloured flowers or for separating groups of rich colour. A few handsome sorts are the following : Madame Chereau, white with violet markings ; florentina, white with lavender tinge ; Mrs. Reuthe, pale lavender ; Standard Bearer, rose, purple and white ; Maori King, yellow and crimson ; Gracchus, lemon yellow with purple markings ; Blue Boy, light blue and purple ; and the common purple kind (Iris germanica). During recent years many novelties have been introduced, some of which are very expensive. In soil deficient in lime these Irises are not usually satisfactory.

Kniphofia (Torch Lily).—There must be one or two plants or groups of Kniphofia (Tritoma) in every flower border for their flaming spires of colour in late summer and autumn. Though generally their cultivation offers no difficulty, on heavy ill-drained ground they are apt to die off or deteriorate in winter. The sites for them should be prepared by taking out large holes and putting in some rubble for drainage if thought necessary. A protection of ashes or leaves round about them provides useful winter protection in cold localities. The leaves, even though they become untidy, should not be trimmed off until early spring. There are many handsome kinds ; for example, aloides, the common Torch Lily, orange red, 4 to 5 feet ; Nelsoni, yellow, 2 to 3 feet ; Tuckii, red and yellow, 4 feet ; nobilis, orange red, 5 to 6 feet ; Lemon Queen, lemon yellow, 5 feet.

Lavandula (Lavender).—A few bushes of Lavender add to the charm of the mixed border, but they must be placed where they are not likely to be crowded by other plants ; if that happens they become bare and lose attractiveness ; it is best to keep them well towards the front of the

CHIEF HARDY FLOWERS

border. A variety to be recommended is called the Munstead Lavender; it is of lower growth than the common kind and flowers earlier.

Lavatera (Tree Mallow).—One of the Tree Mallows, Lavatera Olbia, is a particularly handsome plant, reaching

Flowers of the Bush Mallow (Lavatera Olbia)

a height of 5 to 6 feet, and suitable for the back of the border. It produces a long succession of rose-pink Mallow-like flowers during the summer months. It makes vigorous and rapid growth, and needs plenty of room. It should be cut back in spring.

Linaria (Toadflax).—The most useful of the perennial Toadflaxes for the flower border is Linaria dalmatica (macedonica). It grows to a height of 3 to 4 feet, and bears yellow flowers with orange lip. It is, however, liable to perish after flowering.

Linum (Flax).—The blue Flaxes are dainty and graceful plants; they grow some 18 inches to 2 feet high, and are suitable for placing towards the front of the border. The best kinds are Linum narbonense and L. perenne, both having blue flowers. They thrive best in well-drained soil.

Lobelia.—The herbaceous perennial Lobelias are distinguished in some cases by handsome leaves and in all cases by brilliant flowers. They grow from 2 to 3 or 4 feet high, and thrive best in deep moist soil and partial shade. Although the roots may be left out for the winter in some gardens, it is necessary in most places to lift them in autumn and store them safe from frost for the winter. Some of the best are Queen Victoria, reddish bronze leaves and scarlet flowers; Gloire de St. Anne's, crimson scarlet; fulgens, bronze-red leaves and scarlet flowers; Firefly, crimson scarlet; and Sam Barlow, bronze-green leaves, rose-pink flowers. They are in full beauty in late summer.

Lupinus (Lupin).—The Lupins need no words of praise; they are well known and indispensable flowering plants of early summer. The only thing that can be urged against them is that after the flowering season is past they are somewhat untidy, though the remedy is to cut down the stems, really a beneficial practice, for it prevents the formation of seed pods and encourages the plants to bloom again in autumn. The modern varieties are great improvements upon those formerly grown, and the range of colour has been considerably extended. Some of the most striking are Somerset, yellow; Taplow Purple, purple; Moerheimi, pink; and Butterfly, purple and white, together with the common blue and white varieties. If a packet of seed of Downer's Lupins is obtained and sown in May or June, out of doors, plants bearing flowers of various colours will result, and they will blossom freely the following year.

Lychnis (Campion).—The finest of the border Lychnises is the old Jerusalem Sage (Lychnis chalcedonica), which grows 2 to 3 feet high, and bears heads of scarlet blooms. Lychnis Haageana, obtainable in various colours, is also useful and showy, the flowers being larger than those of Lychnis chalcedonica, but the plants are not such good perennials. Lychnis Viscaria, growing about 12 inches high, and bearing red flowers, is suitable for planting near the front of the border. Lychnis (Agrostemma) coronaria is an accommodating plant, 2 to 3 feet high, with grey leaves and rose-red flowers.

Lythrum (Loosestrife).—The common Loosestrife is a familiar wild flower and one of the showiest of all. Among garden varieties of Loosestrife there are several handsome border plants. They need an abundance of water during the summer months and do best in partial shade, where they are not likely to suffer from drought. Lythrum virgatum Rose Queen, 3 feet, rose, and Lythrum Salicaria splendens, 5 feet, rose purple, are two of the finest sorts.

Malva (Mallow).—The individual flowers of this Mallow are short lived, but a succession of bloom is maintained for some weeks. The plants thrive best in full sunshine and in well-drained soil. The Musk Mallow (Malva moschata), rose, and its white variety are two of the best Mallows for the border. They grow 2 to 3 feet high, and bloom in July.

Mimulus (Musk).—The Monkey Musks, which reach a height of 18 inches or so, are very showy summer flowering plants, and last in beauty for a long time, providing they are in moist soil in partial shade, or alternatively, are kept well supplied with water in dry weather. Various highly coloured forms have been raised between Mimulus luteus and M. cupreus, and they are certainly well worth planting.

Monarda (Bee Balm).—This is an old-fashioned plant, forming a low mass of fragrant foliage, and in summer producing heads of dark-red flowers on stems some 2 feet high. The variety called Cambridge Scarlet has flowers of richer colour, and should be planted in preference to the typical kind.

Nepeta (Catmint).— Nepeta Mussinii is a charming border plant with grey leaves, and in summer produces a profusion of spikes of lavender-blue flowers; the plants remain in beauty for many weeks and are unsurpassed for grouping towards the front of the border, or even for use as an edging. They should be trimmed well back in spring. Nepeta macrantha, which grows about 3 feet high, is also attractive when in full bloom; the flowers are of lavender blue colour.

Oenothera (Evening Primrose).—Although some of the Evening Primroses are of rather untidy appearance and scarcely worth a place among choice border plants, several are well worth growing. Fraseri, golden yellow; fruticosa major, deep yellow; and speciosa, white, are to be recommended.

Paeonia (Paeony).—In a large flower border Paeonies should certainly be planted, but in one of only moderate extent it is doubtful if it is wise to include them. They flower rather early and have an untidy appearance when the leaves are fading. They are, however, among the most handsome flowering plants, and if it is thought that room can be spared they should certainly be included. There are innumerable garden varieties and a selection of colours may be made from any hardy plant catalogue. These plants need deep and rich soil if they are to do well, and they should be left undisturbed.

Papaver (Poppy).—The large, handsome flowers of the varieties of the Oriental Poppy (Papaver orientale) make a gorgeous display in May and June, and the mixed flower border at that season owes much to them. They are easily grown in ordinary soil providing they are left undisturbed. As they are rather unattractive when the flowering season

CHIEF HARDY FLOWERS 131

is over, they should be so placed that later blooming plants will hide them as far as possible. They reach a height, when in bloom, of 2 to 3 feet, and the flowers may be crimson, scarlet, rose, white, salmon and other shades. A few of the most striking are Taplow Scarlet, Jeannie Mawson, salmon, Perry's White.

Pentstemon.—Although the Pentstemon is generally raised from cuttings in September, and planted afresh every spring, in some light well-drained soils they are perennial. The finest flowers are, however, obtained by raising them every year. They are easily grown from seeds sown under glass in early spring. Of named varieties Newbury Gem, Southgate Gem and George Horne, bright red, are striking.

Phlox.—For colour in late July and August the mixed border must rely largely upon the modern varieties of the herbaceous Phlox paniculata. The plants vary in height from 2 feet or so to 4 feet high, and the colours range from white through lilac to purple and through pink to red and crimson. Phloxes need deep rich soil which will ensure the roots being kept moist in dry, hot weather. A partially shaded position is also desirable. They will thrive well on a border facing north in the southern counties. After three years or so the plants usually begin to get thin in the centre, and it becomes necessary to lift and divide them; care must be taken to replant the outer portions only, for they are the more vigorous. Some of the modern varieties are exceptionally handsome, and a selection might well be made from the following: Coquelicot, orange red; Etna, orange red; Iris, deep purple; Cyrano, mauve; Miss Willmott, pale salmon; G. A. Strohlein, orange red; E. Danzanvilliers, pale violet; Sheriff Ivory, carmine rose; W. Watson, pale rose pink; Violet Guest, salmon orange; Elizabeth Campbell, pure salmon; Evangeline, deep salmon.

Physalis (Winter Cherry).—This curious plant is grown for the sake of its enlarged calyces, which colour brilliantly in autumn, then becoming orange red. They are often used

A Flower Bed filled with Phlox

for winter decoration in the home, though their value in the border is not negligible. The two best sorts are Physalis Franchetti and P. Bunyardii; they reach a height of 2 feet or so, and should be grouped towards the front of the border. These plants thrive best in rather light soil.

Polemonium (Jacob's Ladder).—Several of these old flowers are indispensable to the proper furnishing of the border; the plants have attractive, deeply cut leaves, and the flowers are blue. One of the finest is Polemonium Himalayanum, which reaches a height of 3 feet and blooms during June and July; other useful sorts are Richardsonii, 18 inches, and caeruleum, 2 feet. There are also white flowered varieties of the two last named.

Polygonatum (Solomon's Seal).—The graceful, arching stems of this plant, when studded with their pretty greenish white flowers in May, are very decorative. Solomon's Seal thrives best in a shady position, and it may not therefore be thought worth while to plant it in a sunny border; nevertheless it is useful for providing early flowers. Its botanical name is Polygonatum multiflorum.

Polygonum (Knot Grass).—Many of the Polygonums are of rank growth and spread rapidly, often becoming a nuisance, and thus are scarcely suitable for planting in a border of choice flowering plants. But an exception may be made of Polygonum Bistorta, which grows about 2 feet high, and in September bears spikes of pretty rose-coloured flowers.

Potentilla (Potentil). — The showy, Strawberry-like flowers in many bright colours of the modern varieties of Potentilla render these plants indispensable for the mixed border. They reach a height of about 18 inches, and should therefore be grouped near the front of the border. Their flowering season is from June to August. The most striking of all are the varieties William Rollinson, red and orange; Gibson's Scarlet, bright scarlet and a most telling colour; Le Vesuve, crimson and yellow; and Gold Prince, golden yellow. Many other varieties are described in catalogues.

J

Primula (Primrose).—A few groups of the common Primrose and Polyanthus are useful for providing spring flowers in odd corners, and room might well be found for a few of the Japanese Primroses, varieties of Primula japonica, which grow 18 to 24 inches or more high, and produce whorls of variously coloured flowers in the month of May. All these Primroses prefer partial shade and deep, moist soil. They are easily raised from seed sown in a box of soil in a frame in spring, and they will flower the following year if planted out in autumn.

Pulmonaria (Lungwort).—Borage-like plants, growing about 12 inches high, and flowering in spring; the leaves are also decorative. A common name for these plants is "Soldiers and Sailors," because in several kinds the flowers are blue when first they open, and as they fade they become rose coloured. Angustifolia, blue, is one of the best.

Pyrethrum.—Among the border flowers of early summer few are more decorative than the Pyrethrums with their large, single or double Marguerite-like flowers in many charming shades of colour. The disadvantage of these plants is that in heavy soil they are liable to perish in winter, but on well-drained ground they are admirable border plants. They reach a height of 18 to 24 inches, and bloom chiefly in May and June; the flowers are most useful for cutting. Many varieties, from white to crimson, are listed in catalogues.

Rosemarinus (Rosemary).—There should be a few bushes of Rosemary in every garden, and towards the front of the mixed border is a suitable place for them. When they are not in bloom their leaves are attractive, and their fragrance alone justifies their inclusion. Rosemary thrives best in rather light soil, though it is not over particular, and even heavy ground is rendered suitable by adding grit freely. The lilac-coloured flowers are at their best in early summer. When the bushes become unshapely they should be cut back as soon as the flowers are over.

CHIEF HARDY FLOWERS

Rudbeckia (Coneflower).—Late flowering plants with yellow, Daisy-like flowers, with raised centres. A few kinds ought to be grown because they bring colour to the border at a time when most summer flowers are past. A few of the best are Golden Glow, double flowers, 6 to 7 feet; maxima, 6 to 7 feet; and speciosa, 2 feet.

Salvia (Sage).—The finest hardy Sage for the flower border is Salvia virgata nemorosa; it grows 2 to 3 feet high, and in July and August is smothered in showy violet blue flowers, then making a delightful display. It looks best when planted near grey-leaved plants, which serve to show off the flowers to the best advantage. Salvia patens, a tuberous rooted, half hardy plant which bears intense blue flowers in late summer, is very beautiful; it grows about 20 inches high. The roots must be lifted and stored in a box of soil in a frost-proof place for the winter.

Santolina (Lavender Cotton).—This is of value for its attractive grey leaves; it reaches a height of 18 to 24 inches, and soon forms a large bush. Santolina incana and S. Chamaecyparissus are the two chief kinds. Grey-leaved plants are of great value in the border when this is arranged as a colour scheme, for they serve to separate shades that might otherwise clash and to show off to advantage some of the richly coloured blooms.

Scabiosa (Scabious).—The chief perennial Scabious is S. caucasica; this plant reaches a height of 2 feet or so, and bears large and beautiful lilac mauve flowers. Unfortunately it is not a reliable perennial on heavy ground, though on light, well-drained land it passes through the winter safely. It may be raised from seed sown in spring to provide flowering plants for the following year.

Sedum (Stonecrop).—The most useful of the Stonecrops for the flower border is Sedum spectabile, a Japanese plant about 18 inches high, with grey leaves and bearing large flat heads of rose purple flowers; the variety atrosanguinea has flowers of more striking and deeper colour. This Stonecrop is at its best late in August and in September, and is an ideal plant for the front of the border.

Sidalcea (Grecian Mallow).—These plants grow 3 to 4 feet high, and are at their best in July, when they bear Mallow-like flowers on tall, graceful stems. The best kinds are Sidalcea Listeri, rose pink, and Rosy Gem of richer colour. Sidalcea candida has white flowers.

Sisyrinchium (Satin Flower).—Choice Iris-like plants, of which one or two are of value for the mixed border. They need rather light soil to do really well, and if a little peat or leaf-mould is mixed in at planting time so much the better. The most useful kinds are Sisyrinchium grandiflorum, 12 inches, purple flowers in April and May; Bermudianum, 12 to 15 inches, blue flowers in May and June; and striatum, 2 feet, yellow flowers in May and June.

Solidago (Golden Rod).—Useful yellow flowering plants that are at their best in late summer and autumn. The small blooms are produced in graceful sprays. Some of the chief kinds are Shortii, 5 feet; canadensis, 4 feet; and Golden Wings, 5 feet. They bloom in August and September.

Spiraea.—Providing they are planted in deep, moist soil, or alternatively are kept well supplied with water in summer, several of the Spiraeas are valuable border flowers. The most handsome of all the herbaceous perennials is Spiraea Aruncus, a noble plant reaching a height of 5 feet or so and bearing large plumes of cream white flowers in July and August. Spiraea filipendula and S. Ulmaria (Meadow Sweet) are attractive, white-flowered plants growing 18 inches high.

Statice (Sea Lavender).—The perennial Sea Lavenders have large, evergreen leaves, and in late summer bear panicles of small, graceful flowers that are very decorative, and useful to cut for winter use in the home. They are best suited by rather light soil. The most striking kind is Statice latifolia, which reaches a height of 2 feet or so, and has lavender

CHIEF HARDY FLOWERS

blue flowers which are at their best in August and September. Statice incana, 12 inches, reddish flowers in August and September, and Gmelini, purple flowers in August and September, 18 inches high, are other useful Statices.

Thalictrum (Meadow Rue).—The Meadow Rues are particularly graceful and decorative plants, with attractive leaves and in summer conspicuous inflorescences of yellow, purple and other shades. They need deep and fairly rich soil if they are to be seen at their best. Aquilegifolium, 3 feet, purple, June; flavum, 3 to 4 feet, yellow, June; and dipterocarpum, 5 feet, mauve, August and September, are some of the finest kinds.

Trollius (Globe Flower).—Familiar garden flowers which have long been in cultivation. They grow from 2 to 3 feet high, and make a brave show in April and May, when the globe-shaped flowers of yellow or orange colouring are at their best. They need moist soil, and a partially shaded position is most suitable. The chief kinds are asiaticus, 15 to 18 inches, yellow, May; europaeus, 18 inches, lemon yellow, May; Golden Globe, 2 feet, golden yellow, May.

Verbascum (Mullein).—Most of the Mulleins are biennials, and must be raised fresh from seed each spring to provide flowering plants for the summer following, but there are several good perennial kinds. Perhaps the best of these is Verbascum densiflorum, which reaches a height of 5 feet or so, and is in full beauty in July, when its tall stems are clothed with yellow flowers. V. Chaixii is another good perennial Mullein; it grows 3 feet high and bears yellow flowers. V. nigrum, 3 feet, yellow, and V. phoeniceum, with variously coloured flowers, are others worth planting. All bloom in July.

Verbena.—One of the most striking of all Verbenas is that named venosa; from July onwards it is a mass of purple flowers, and makes a brilliant patch of colour towards the front of the border. The plants only grow some 15 inches high. Unfortunately this Verbena is not thoroughly hardy, though on light, well-drained land in southern gardens it usually passes through the winter safely.

Veronica (Speedwell).—There are several charming

A Handsome Perennial Mullein (Verbascum densiflorum)

hardy flowers among the Speedwells; they are distinguished by fairly tall and graceful stems, and bear small flowers of some shade of blue. Gentianoides, 18 inches, bears pale blue flowers in May; longifolia, 2 to 3 feet, has blue flowers in August (there are varieties with white and rose coloured flowers); virginica, with blue flowers on stems 3 to 4 feet high, is at its best in July.

Viola.—Tufted Pansies or Violas are particularly useful as an edging to the mixed flower border. If the old flowers are picked off the plants blossom throughout the summer months. When they become untidy and straggling the long shoots should be cut off, leaving compact tufts which will again bloom in a few weeks' time. It is best to raise fresh plants each September from cuttings, keeping these in a frame during the winter; they will be ready for planting out of doors in spring. The old plants, if left undisturbed, produce a profusion of blossom in spring and early summer, but their display does not persist so late in the season as that of the young plants. Some of the best varieties are White Swan, white; Primrose Dame, light yellow; Royal Sovereign, golden yellow; Maggie Mott, lilac mauve; J. B. Riding, reddish mauve.

Many hardy perennials may be propagated by means of cuttings inserted in pots or boxes of sandy soil, and placed in a frame for a few weeks. The frame must be kept closed, except that a little air needs to be admitted for half an hour or so each morning to get rid of any moisture that has accumulated. If the pots or boxes of cuttings are once watered through a can having a fine " rose " on the spout, the soil can be moistened sufficiently, until the cuttings are rooted, by syringeing them daily in fine weather. A suitable length for most cuttings is 3 to 4 inches, and they are prepared by removing a few of the lowest leaves and cutting the stem immediately below a joint. It is an excellent plan to scatter sand on the soil before the cuttings are put in, so that some of it falls to the bottom of the holes. The soil must be pressed firmly to the base of the cuttings by means of a small stick.

When taking cuttings from the plants it is often possible to detach pieces which already possess a few roots; these, of course, make quicker progress than unrooted cuttings, and should be chosen if available.

Those plants which form large clumps consisting of numerous shoots, such as Michaelmas Daisy and Helenium, may be increased by cuttings in spring ; so too may Phlox, Delphinium, Border Chrysanthemum, and others of similar growth. Such plants as Pinks, Sun Rose (Helianthemum) Iberis (Evergreen Candytuft), Aubrietia and Alyssum are increased by cuttings taken as soon as the flower display is past.

Viola, Pansy, Snapdragon, Pentstemon, Hollyhock and Lavender are propagated by cuttings in August and September, and at that time cuttings are also taken of half-hardy bedding plants, which are sometimes used to add colour to the mixed flower border.

INDEX

ACANTHUS, 104
Achillea, 23, 104
Aconitum, 104; Wilsoni, 59
Alkanet, 105
Alstroemeria, 104
Althaea, 104
Alum root, 125
Alyssum, 23, 105
Anchusa, 105; Dropmore, 59; Opal, 59; propagating by root cuttings, 106
Anemone, Japanese, 106
Annual flowers, a border of, 94
Annuals for the blue border, 59; for the red border, 93; some of the best, 94; staking, 18
Antennaria, 24
Anthemis, 106; Kelwayi, 80
Antirrhinums, yellow, 85
Aquilegia, 33
Arabis, double white, 106
Armeria, 106
Arranging and grouping, 9
Artemisia, 106; Abrotanum, 24
Artificial manure, 15; for the border, best, 15
Aster, Mrs. J. F. Rayner, 93; perennial, 108
Asters, mauve, 73
Astilbe, 109
Astilbes, rose-coloured, 79
Aubrietia, 109
Autumn flowers in the mixed border, 48
Avens, 120

BACKGROUND of flower border, 45
Basic slag, 15
Bee Balm, 129
Bellflower, 109; The Chimney, 33
Bergamot, 91
Biennials for the border, 33; sowing seeds of, 34
Bleeding Heart, 116
Blue flower border, 54; flowers in spring, 54; flowers in summer, 54

Bocconia, 109
Border Chrysanthemum, Goacher's Crimson, 93; flower, extending the season of, 48; how to prepare, 6; of annual flowers, 94; suitable width of flower, 2; the mixed flower, 1
Bulbs in the flower border, 28; where to plant, 28
Burning Bush, 91, 116

CAMPANULA, 109
Campion, 129
Candytuft, Evergreen, 125
Canterbury Bell, 33; rose, 79
Carnation, 110; Border, 114; Perpetual, 116; perpetual Border, 116
Catananche, 110
Catmint, 130
Centaurea, 112
Centranthus, 112
Cerastium tomentosum, 20
Chamomile, 106
Cherry, Winter, 131
Chief hardy border flowers, 104
Chrysanthemum, Border, 112; Goacher's Crimson, 93; maximum, 68, 112
Cimicifuga, 113
Clary, the Silvery, 20
Clematis for background to blue border, 54
Climbing plants in the mixed border, 2
Colour associations, 48; effect, planting for, 45
Coneflower, 86, 135; purple, 117
Coreopsis, 113
Cornflowers, 59
Cultivation, 13
Cupidone, 110
Cutting down perennials in autumn, 18
Cuttings of perennials, 139

INDEX

DAHLIAS, 86; for the red border, 93
Daisies, Shasta, 112
Delphinium, 114; a white, 68
Delphiniums, 58; mauve, 69
Dianthus. 114; Allwoodii, 114; caesius, 24
Dicentra, 116
Dictamnus, 116; Fraxinella, 91
Division, increasing perennials by, 40
Doronicum, 80, 116

ECHINACEA purpurea, 117
Echinops, 59, 117
Edging plants, 20; how to arrange, 20; selection of, 12
Eremurus, 32
Erigeron, 118; speciosus, 69
Eryngium. 59, 118
Evening Primrose, 130
Everlasting Flower, 96

FLAX, 128
Fleabane, 113
Flower border, the mixed, 1; extending the season of blossom, 48
Flowers, planting hardy, 6; from seed, hardy, 36; easily raised from seed, 39
Foreground of flower border, 47
Forget-me-nots, 54
Forsythia spectabilis, 100; intermedia, 100
Foxglove, 33
Fuchsia, Hardy, 103
Funkia, 118

GAILLARDIA, 81, 120
Galega, 120
Gauze Flower, 123
Geum, 120; Mrs. Bradshaw, 87
Gladioli, 32
Globe Flower, 137
Globe Thistle, 117
Goat's Beard, 109
Goat's Rue, 120
Godetia, 96
Golden Bell shrub, 100
Golden Rod, 136
Grey-leaved plants, 23
Grouping and arranging, 9; hardy plants, 3; mistakes in, 9
Groups, number of plants in, 11
Gypsophila, 123

HAMAMELIS mollis, 100
Hardy flowers from seeds, 36; planting, 6
Helenium, 123; Riverton Beauty, 86; Riverton Gem, 86
Helianthemum, 24, 123
Helianthus, 125
Hemerocallis, 125
Herbaceous perennial, a, 1
Heuchera, 125; sanguinea, 87
Hollyhock, 104
Honesty, 33
Hyacinth, Grape, 100; the Cape, 32
Hyacinthus candicans, 32

IBERIS, 125
Increasing perennials by cuttings, 139; perennials by division, 40
Iris, 126; aurea, 85; English, 28; Flag, 126; germanica, 73; Spanish, 28

JACOB'S Ladder, 133

KNAPWEED, 112
Kniphofia, 91, 126; yellow kinds, 85
Knot Grass, 133

LARKSPUR, 114
Laurustinus, 103
Lavandula, 126
Lavatera, 127
Lavender, 25, 126; Cotton, 135; Sea, 136
Leaf-mould, value of, 13
Leopard's Bane, 116
Lilies for the flower border, 30
Lilium candidum. 30; croceum, 31; elegans, 31; Henryi, 31; pardalinum, 31; speciosum, 30; testaceum, 31; Thunbergianum, 31
Lily, Day, 125; Herb, 104; Peruvian, 104; Plantain, 118; Torch, 126
Linaria, 128
Linum, 128
Lobelia cardinalis, 93; perennial, 128
Loosestrife, 129
Lungwort, 134
Lupin, 59, 128; yellow, 86
Lupinus, 128; roseus, 79
Lychnis, 129; chalcedonica, 91; coronaria, 26
Lythrum, 129

INDEX

MADWORT, 105
Mallow, 129; Grecian, 136; Tree, 127
Malva, 129
Manure, when to apply, 13
Manures, artificial, applying, 15
Manuring, 13
Marigolds, 96
Mauve flower border, 69
Meadow Rue, 137
Michaelmas Daisies, the best, 108; white, 68
Michaelmas Daisy, 61
Mimulus, 129; cardinalis, 87
Mistakes in grouping, 9
Mock Orange, 101
Monarda, 129; didyma, 91
Monkey Flower, 87
Monkshoods, 59, 104
Montbretia, 93
Mullein, 137
Muscari, Heavenly Blue, 101
Musk, 129

Poppy, the Plume, 109; white, 66
Potentilla, 133
Preparing flower border, 6
Primrose, 134; Evening, 130; Japanese, 134
Primula, 134
Pulmonaria, 134
Pyrethrum, 87, 134

RED flower border, 87
Rhododendron, Pink Pearl, 103
Rose and pink flower border, 74
Rose, Excelsa, 91; Hiawatha, 91; Shower of Gold, 85; Sun 24, 123
Roses, Standard, in the flower border, 103
Rosemary, 134
Rudbeckia, 86, 135

NARCISSI, white-flowered, 66
Nepeta, 130; Mussinii, 26, 73
Nigella, 59
Nitrate of soda, 15

OENOTHERA, 130
"Old Man," 106

PAEONIA, 130
Paeonies, 79, 87, 130
Pansy, tufted, 139
Papaver, 130
Pentstemon, 131
Perennial, a herbaceous, 1
Perennials, cutting down in autumn, 18; increasing by cuttings, 139; increasing by division, 40
Petunia, white, 66
Philadelphus, double, 101
Phlox, 58, 131
Phloxes, mauve, 70; red shades, 91; rose and pink, 79; white, 68
Physalis, 131
Pink and rose flower border, 74
Pink, 114; the Cheddar, 24
Planting for colour effect, 45; hardy flowers, 6
Plants for edging, 20
Polemonium, 133
Polyanthus, 33
Polygonatum, 133
Polygonum, 133
Poppies, Oriental, 130; red and scarlet, 91; perennial, 79

SALVIA, 135; argentea, 26; patens, 29, 59
Santolina, 135
Satin Flower, 136
Saxifraga, 26
Scabiosa pterocephala, 26
Scabious, 135
Sea Holly, 118
Sea Lavender, 69, 136
Sedum, 26, 135
Seeds of hardy flowers, sowing, 36
Shrubs for the flower border, 100
Sidalcea, 136
Sisyrinchium, 136
Snapdragons, yellow, 85
Sneezewort, 123
Solidago, 136
Solomon's Seal, 133
Speedwell, 138
Spiraea, 136; Anthony Waterer, 103; Thunbergii, 103
Spring flowers in the mixed border, 48; work on the border, 15
Stachys lanata, 27
Staking, 16; various methods of, 16
Starwort, Summer, 118
Statice, 136; latifolia, 69
Stocks, 66, 94
Stonecrop, 26, 135
Sulphate of ammonia, 15
Sunflower, perennial, 125
Superphosphate of lime, 15
Supports for slender plants, 16; for vigorous plants, 17
Sweet Peas, blue, 59; mauve, 73; pale yellow, 86; pink and rose, 74; red, 91
Sweet Sultan, 73
Sweet William, 33; Pink Beauty, 74

INDEX

THALICTRUM, 137
Thrift, 106
Thyme, Ornamental, 27
Tickseed, 113
Toadflax, 128
Top-dressing, value of, 13
Trollius, 85, 137
Tulips, mauve, 69; red, 87; rose and pink, 74; white, 66
Tying, 16

VALERIAN, 112
Verbascum, 137; Miss Willmott, 66; olympicum, 81

Verbena, 137; white, 66
Veronica, 138; incana, 27
Viola, 139

WALLFLOWER, 33; Cloth of Gold, 80; reddish, 87
White flower border, 62
Windflower, 106
Winter Cherry, 131
Witch Hazel, 100
Wormwood, 106

YELLOW flower border, 80

Printed in Great Britain
by Amazon